Sherman

THE GREAT GENERALS SERIES

This distinguished new series features the lives of eminent military leaders who changed history in the United States and abroad. Top military historians write concise but comprehensive biographies including the personal lives, battles, strategies, and legacies of these great generals, with the aim to provide background and insight into today's armies and wars. These books are of interest to the military history buff, and, thanks to fast-paced narratives and references to current affairs, they are also accessible to the general reader.

Sherman

Steven E. Woodworth

palgrave

SHERMAN
Copyright © Steven E. Woodworth, 2009.
All rights reserved.

First published in 2009 by PALGRAVE MACMILLAN® in the
US—a division of St. Martin's Press LLC, 175 Fifth Avenue, New
York, NY 10010.

Where this book is distributed in the UK, Europe and the rest of
the world, this is by Palgrave Macmillan, a division of Macmillan
Publishers Limited, registered in England, company number
785998, of Houndmills, Basingstoke, Hampshire RG21 6XS.

Palgrave Macmillan is the global academic imprint of the above
companies and has companies and representatives throughout the
world.

Palgrave® and Macmillan® are registered trademarks in the United
States, the United Kingdom, Europe and other countries.

ISBN-13: 978-0-230-61024-8
ISBN-10: 0-230-61024-2

All images appear courtesy of the Library of Congress

Library of Congress Cataloging-in-Publication Data
Woodworth, Steven E.
   Sherman / Steven E. Woodworth ; foreword by Wesley K. Clark.
     p. cm.
   Includes bibliographical references and index.
   ISBN 0-230-61024-2
   1. Sherman, William T. (William Tecumseh), 1820–1891. 2.
Generals—United States—Biography. 3. United States. Army—
Biography. 4. United States—History—Civil War, 1861–1865—
Campaigns. I. Title.
E467.1.S55W83 2008
355.0092—dc22
[B]

                           2008022060

A catalogue record of the book is available from the British Library.

Design by Letra Libre

First edition: January 2009
10 9 8 7 6 5 4 3 2 1
Printed in the United States of America.

For Nathan, Jonathan, David, Daniel,
Anna, Elizabeth, and Mary.

To God alone by the glory.

Acknowledgments

I TAKE PLEASURE IN ACKNOWLEDGING WITH GRATITUDE the assistance of Alessandra Bastagli and Emma Hamilton of Palgrave Macmillan. Carl Schenker supplied me with a number of useful items of information, including a copy of his excellent article on Sherman's given name. Noah Andre Trudeau provided helpful comments on the manuscript. Charles Grear gave his gracious permission for the use of the maps contained in this volume. To all of these individuals, I am very grateful.

Contents

Photosection appears between pages 104 and 105

Foreword

IN THE OLD SOUTH, HIS NAME STILL EVOKES A CURSE, DISLIKE, and even a little fear. In the Army, he is known as Grant's most loyal and effective lieutenant. And in most of America, mention his name and you may get a quizzical response, "Someone from the Civil War?"

Oh, yes, General William Tecumseh Sherman was indeed someone from the Civil War. He was the second most famous of the Union generals, and a man who used his skill and insight not only to blaze a trail of destruction across the American South but also to create a new form of maneuver, a "strategy of the indirect."

Innovation in war is usually accidental—a combination of necessity, insight and something different in the circumstances—technology, terrain, or enemy organization—in which war is conducted. Confronting a stubborn enemy, lacking an overwhelming superiority in numbers, failing time and again in direct assault, Union Army General William "Cump" Sherman became just such an innovator. The emergence of this stratagem is at the heart of Steven Woodworth's fast-paced biography.

Sherman's childhood was marked by the early misfortune of losing his father and being taken in by a well-to-do family. In fact, Sherman was raised in a relatively prosperous Midwestern home with considerable opportunities. He selected the Army, chose to go to West Point, and through political connections, received his appointment. Sherman was a good student and passable cadet, and in 1840 he was commissioned into the artillery branch.

But in the Army, as in life, luck plays a major role. And "Cump" Sherman had none of it early on. While he proved an able junior officer, he missed the crucible of the Mexican War. Seemingly consigned to insignificant postings in Florida, California, Missouri, and Louisiana, and with his wife troubled by the Army's frugal lifestyle, he left the service in 1851 to try his hand in business. But the 1850s were a time of considerable financial turmoil and despite Sherman's considerable personal talents as a banker, his bank foundered. He ended up heading a military school in Louisiana—only to resign with the rise of secessionist activities in Louisiana.

As war approached Sherman offered his services and was appointed a colonel of infantry, commanding first a regiment, then a brigade. And now he was, at last, in the thick of the fight.

Sherman learned command in war the only way it can be learned—by experience. His brigade fought at the first Battle of Bull Run. Promoted to Brigadier General in the expanding Union army, he was chosen to serve in Kentucky, and after a few weeks assumed command of Union forces there. And here, in the ruse and feint of the border states, Sherman nearly lost his way. Overreacting to enemy pressures, excitable and insecure, his extreme statements soon made him the target for public criticism. He was reassigned, and given some rest. But he had struck up a relationship of sorts with a fellow department commander, a young man in Missouri named Ulysses Grant. It was a relationship that over time would win the war, forge a nation, and change warfare.

From early 1862 Sherman came to serve as Grant's most trusted, loyal and capable subordinate. Sherman was tested as a division commander at the bloody Battle of Shiloh, where he proved strong and steady in a tough, confusing fight. And while Grant suffered the blame for the high losses, and the envy for his victory, Sherman somehow managed to hang on, just below the horizon of jealousy from his fellow generals.

During the spring and summer he worked in western Tennessee, with its railroad, guerrilla fighters, and the disconsolate civil populace, and was promoted to command the district. By late 1862, he was again teamed up with Grant, working on the problem of Vicksburg. The Confederate strong-point effectively blocked Union use of the Mississippi and helped to unite the Confederacy on an east-west axis. Six months of maneuver, march, and countermarch followed, with Sherman rising to the fore as Grant's most able commander, while Grant himself struggled with the strategy and tactics to take down Vicksburg.

For Sherman, it must have been a period of intense personal growth, as he saw again and again the interplay of enemy threats, capabilities, and intent with his own actions, and he learned to protect and sustain his forces within a hostile population. But it was also a period when Sherman cemented his reputation with the troops through his sheer personal competence and presence on the battlefield. Whether it was demonstrating the proper way to construct a fascine, or showing up at the front personally to reconnoiter, Sherman earned his men's trust and admiration not just as a distant, heroic personality, but also as someone with enormous personal competence.

After the fall of Vicksburg in July 1863, Sherman remained at work in the western theater, and then advanced in authority to command the Union's Army of the Tennessee. Under Grant's leadership, he moved to rescue a Union force besieged in Chattanooga, breaking the siege and defeating Confederate forces in the area in late 1863. Then, he launched the campaigns that made him famous and ended the war: he broke the South. Literally. Marching away from supply lines, avoiding combat on unfavorable terms, foraging for his own sustenance, and denying it to the enemy, he cut through America— Mississippi, Alabama, northern Georgia. He captured Atlanta and marched to the sea at Savannah. Along the way he destroyed the war-making potential of the South. By the time he marched up through the Carolinas to link up with Grant, the outcome was decided. The South was beaten.

Grant fought to crush Lee's Army; Sherman fought to break the support base that sustained the resistance. And with this indirect approach, Sherman opened a new vision into the conduct of warfare. Later, with the advent of the machine gun, artillery, and aircraft, future generations of military leaders would ask themselves if there wasn't a way of avoiding the big battles, of breaking the enemy through indirect maneuver. And they looked back, always, to Sherman to find the answer.

But to the generals of the U.S. Army, "Cump" Sherman symbolizes also the great teamwork of two fighting generals, and the great trust, loyalty, and resolve that made it possible. Ultimately, the spirit of this teamwork may have been Sherman's most enduring gift to the United States Army.

Introduction

THE VIEW FROM KENNESAW MOUNTAIN WAS SPECTACULAR. In the crystal-clear air of a crisp autumn morning, from this perch a thousand feet above the surrounding terrain, the eye could range for miles. Looking north from the summit, General William Tecumseh Sherman could see all of northwest Georgia spread out below him in a washboard series of ridges. But Sherman had not come to admire the view. He was anxious and fretful as he scanned the terrain for telltale signs of the presence of his own or the enemy's troops. The military situation was not to his liking. A little more than one month earlier he had scored the greatest Union success of 1864 by capturing the city of Atlanta, but while he had conferred by telegraph with his superiors about what his army's next move should be, the enemy had moved first. The always-aggressive Confederate general John Bell Hood had turned Sherman's position in Atlanta, maneuvering in a wide arc around it on the west. From this position, the Rebel commander was now threatening to cut Sherman's supply line to the north.

Sherman knew all about turning maneuvers. In the campaign that had taken him to Atlanta, Sherman had executed more and bigger turning maneuvers than any previous campaign in this war— more than opposing commanders had thought possible. Again and again he had refused to attack the enemy's strong defensive positions. Only here, at this very mountain, three months ago, had he succumbed to impatience and launched a major frontal assault. The result had been 3,000 casualties and nothing was gained but a grim lesson. Through the rest of the campaign he had maneuvered around every Confederate strongpoint to find the weaknesses that would force his opponent either to retreat or to offer headlong battle under conditions that would favor Sherman. He had done it to Joseph Johnston on the very ground he now surveyed, and Johnston had chosen retreat every time—until Confederate president Jefferson Davis had sacked him in favor of the more pugnacious Hood. Then Sherman had turned Hood, and Hood had fought. Four times Sherman had whipped him badly, and the fourth time had left Hood in such an unfavorable position that he had to abandon Atlanta to the victorious Sherman, triggering celebration all across the war-weary North.

And now Hood had turned him. The Confederate army was this very morning between Sherman and the Union base of supplies, threatening to cut the Federals off. Fifteen miles to the west, near the town of Dallas, Sherman could see the smoke of many campfires that could only be those of the enemy—a large portion of Hood's force. Other Confederates had obviously been at work closer to the mountain. From the whistle stop of Big Shanty at the northern foot of Kennesaw, the line of the Western & Atlantic Railroad—the tracks that carried every hardtack cracker Sherman's soldiers ate—was dotted with scores of smoking bonfires, where Rebels had piled and burned the ties to heat and bend the rails thrown across them. At the far end of the line of smokes, fourteen miles north of Kennesaw, rose a thicker cloud of a different kind of smoke. It was not wood, but a great deal of black powder that someone was burning, and Sherman could just make out the rumble of distant cannon. That could only indicate that the Confederates were attacking his supply depot at Allatoona Pass, as he had expected Hood would do once the Confederate got around him.

Sherman worried about the situation at Allatoona. He wondered if the reinforcements he had ordered to join the undersized garrison had arrived before the Confederates. He wondered if the post could hold out. Hood would like nothing better than to deprive Sherman of both his railroad and his supply depot, goading the Union general into making a desperate assault against Hood, whose Confederates were firmly ensconced in the impregnable fastness of Allatoona Gap. Sherman had declined to attack the gap on his way south and had no intention of doing so now, but if the depot fell and Hood gained such a strong position on his supply line, Sherman was going to have to put his men on very short rations indeed.

As the morning passed, so did the crisis at Allatoona. Nearby signalmen informed Sherman that they had contacted the fort at the pass by signal flags and received word that the reinforcements were in place. Sherman could gauge the progress of his relief column by the rising smoke of bonfires he had ordered its commander to have kindled periodically near the head of the column. Then the guns around Allatoona fell silent, and the signal flags fluttered again, sending a message that all was well. A relieved Sherman could turn his thoughts from the immediate crisis to the question of what course he should take against Hood's continued threats to his supply lines.[1]

He was unwilling to continue the game Hood had been playing with him the past week. He would have been happy enough to meet the Rebel in battle on anything like even terrain, but it was clear that Hood, with his smaller and more nimble army, would never allow that to happen. Sherman was determined neither to retreat nor to fight at a disadvantage—the two unpleasant choices he had forced on his opponents. Every other military thinker in the nation, perhaps in the world, would have said he had no alternative. Sherman thought differently.

He had already sketched his idea in letters both to his superior, Ulysses S. Grant, and to his subordinate and old West Point classmate, George H. Thomas. He would use the principle of maneuver in a new way. Rather than maneuvering to gain a tactical advantage on a battlefield or to threaten an enemy army's immediate supply line, he would bypass the enemy's army completely and penetrate deep behind what had been enemy lines, doing massive damage to industry, infrastructure, and morale—everything that enabled the enemy to sustain armies in the field. He would march all the way through Georgia to the sea, tearing the heart out of the Confederacy. No one in Washington could see it yet. Neither could Grant or Thomas, but Sherman was determined to convince them and then make the march and show the world what he could do. As he told a staff officer later that month, "It's a big game, but I can do it—I *know* I can do it."[2]

And so he did. Sherman brought a new dimension to the Civil War and foreshadowed new methods of waging war. This was not, as legend would have it, in the area of destructiveness or of the mistreatment of civilians. Such things had been done before, numberless times over the course of many centuries and with far more intensity and less restraint than Sherman's men practiced, notwithstanding the mythology of vandalism that has grown up around them. Sherman developed what would later be called maneuver warfare to an entirely new level. By the final year of the war he had learned to avoid attacking the enemy's areas of strength, maneuvering instead toward the weakly held areas the enemy could not afford to lose. It was a way of achieving success in war with a minimum of the great battles that made demigods of victorious generals, riding triumphantly over fields carpeted with the enemy's slain and their own. After the fall of Atlanta, Sherman carried his concept farther, maneuvering once again away from the enemy's strength and this time penetrating deep into enemy territory to strike at the opposing society's economic resources and will to resist. It was to make him one of the most celebrated, admired, and hated generals of American history and its basic principles still lie at the heart of the way generals plan campaigns today.

CHAPTER ONE

The Education of a Soldier, 1820–1845

ON A CHILLY WINTER DAY IN LANCASTER, OHIO, CHARLES R. Sherman and his wife Mary Hoyt Sherman welcomed the birth of their sixth child, a boy whom Charles named William Tecumseh, with the middle name honoring Ohio's most celebrated Indian chief. "Tecumseh was a great warrior," the father later explained to non-plussed neighbors. The large and growing Sherman family lived on Main Street in a clapboard house built in the style popular in Charles and Mary's native Connecticut. It marked the Shermans as one of the more distinguished families in this twenty-year-old town where the frontier road, known as Zane's Trace, crossed the Hocking River.[1]

By February 8, 1820, when young "Cump," as his siblings would soon be calling him, made his appearance in the world, Charles Sherman was a successful lawyer. A veteran of the War of

1812, though without seeing combat, Charles rode the judicial circuit. A big, florid, energetic man, he was highly respected, but his family did not enjoy the affluence that his profession and status might have brought. Three years before Tecumseh's birth, Charles had suffered a serious financial disaster. While serving as the U.S. collector of internal revenue for the third district of Ohio, he had accepted various banknotes in payment of taxes and failed to adjust quickly enough to avoid catastrophe when the federal government announced a change of policy, specifying the acceptance of only Bank of the United States notes or coins. As a consequence, Sherman was left with massive amounts of worthless paper money and a crushing debt. Rather than declare bankruptcy, he set out to pay the debt and struggled under the load for the rest of his life.[2]

In 1823, Charles won appointment to the Ohio Supreme Court. In those days, even justices on the state's highest judicial tribunal still rode the circuit, traveling around the state to hold court in various towns, and so he continued to be away from home a good deal of the time. He was on the circuit on June 18, 1829, holding court in Lebanon, Ohio, ninety-five miles from Lancaster, when he was suddenly taken ill with a high fever. Friends brought him to a hotel, summoned a physician, and sent word to Lancaster. Mary Sherman set out at once by coach but had only got as far as Washington Court House, Ohio—when, on June 24, Charles succumbed to what his family ever afterward believed had been typhoid, though others thought it was cholera.[3]

Charles's unexpected death left Mary with the house, the furniture, some bank stock worth about two hundred dollars per year, and eleven children, the youngest just one month old. In its straitened situation, the Sherman household was going to have to get much smaller. The older boys, all the way down to fourteen-year-old Jim, took jobs or apprenticeships and moved out on their own. The oldest girl, sixteen-year-old Elizabeth, married. Relatives and friends took in most of the younger children one by one—five-year-old John to Mount Vernon, Ohio; seven-year-old Lamp to Cincinnati.[4]

Cump stayed in Lancaster and was adopted by a neighbor at the other end of the block. Thomas Ewing, Sr., a close friend of the Sherman family, took the lad to live with his family at the corner of Main and High streets. The Ewing house was large and ornate outside and stocked inside with such finery as fancy china and a piano. The forty-year-old Ewing was equally impressive, "an intellectual giant," Tecumseh would later call him. Ewing had worked his way through college by alternating studies with stints of hard labor at the salt works in Kanawha, Virginia (later West Virginia). After graduation he studied under Lancaster's leading lawyer and gained admission to the bar in 1816. A big, bluff, imposing man at more than six feet and two hundred sixty pounds, Ewing found immediate success in his profession and had the look of a man bound for greater things.[5]

Ewing "looked down on religion as something domestic," Tecumseh would recall. By contrast, Ewing's wife Maria was a devout Catholic who was diligently raising her own four children—Tecumseh's juniors—as well as the two nieces and one nephew who lived in the Ewing household, as good Catholics. When Thomas brought Tecumseh to the Ewing house, Maria decreed that he could remain in her household only if he was baptized into the Roman Catholic faith. As always in matters of religion, Thomas acquiesced. Tecumseh was not consulted. An itinerant Dominican priest, on his next monthly visit to Lancaster, baptized him in the Ewings' front parlor.[6]

And so young Sherman grew up as a foster member of the Ewing family. Thomas had promised to treat him as one of his own, and he was as good as his word. The rest of the family was similarly accepting, and Tecumseh genuinely liked them and felt gratitude for their having taken him in. Yet, he never addressed Thomas and Maria as "Father" or "Mother" but rather as Mr. or Mrs. Ewing. Sherman was bright and obedient but fond of mischief; he was a passable scholar, always near the top of his classes but much more interested in play or even outdoor physical labor than the tedium of the schoolroom. Along with the Ewing children, he attended Sunday mass and received extensive instruction in the Catholic faith with the degree of submission the ever stringent Maria required. From Maria and the priests, he learned Catholic doctrine and liturgy and the the catechism. From his foster father, Tecumseh learned that a real man was quietly disdainful of religion while benevolently tolerating his devout wife's piety. He also learned from Thomas Ewing that slavery was innocuous, blacks were inferior, and abolitionists were repugnant and potentially dangerous.[7]

In the years after Tecumseh joined the household, Ewing continued to rise. In 1830, he won election to the United States Senate as a Whig. Failing in his bid for reelection in 1836, he received an appointment in 1841 as Secretary of the Treasury in the administration of newly-elected President William Henry Harrison.

By that time, Sherman had taken his own path in life. He had been fascinated with the military since the boyhood day he had watched a militia officer drilling amateur soldiers on an open field near Lancaster. Charles Sherman, before his death, had spoken to Thomas Ewing about his desire that Cump should be trained for public service in the army or navy, and Mary Sherman liked the idea of her son as a cadet at West Point better than she did the idea of him as a midshipman in the navy. So, in 1836, when Tecumseh was sixteen and Ewing was still in the Senate, his foster father obtained for him an appointment to the U.S. Military Academy at West Point.[8]

Leaving Lancaster on May 20, 1836, Sherman traveled by stagecoach and train until a steamboat carried him the last leg of his journey up the scenic Hudson River to where the academy sat atop its bluff overlooking the river below. Sherman easily passed the entrance exam and entered into the life of a West Point plebe. He accommodated himself with little complaint to the academy's Spartan rules and living conditions. Midway through his academy years the students' living quarters gained the lavish addition of iron bedsteads, so that the cadets no longer had to sleep on pallets on the floor. Otherwise, each room contained a mirror and washstand, a table, chair, and lamp, and an open fireplace for heat. From reveille at 5:30 A.M. until lights-out at 9:30 P.M., every hour of the cadet's day was precisely regimented—study, lecture, and recitations, punctuated by meals that by all accounts were worse than Spartan—boiled meat, boiled potatoes, boiled pudding, boiled coffee.[9] Sherman coped easily with the stringent academic regimen of West Point and consistently stayed near the top of his class. The academy during the nineteenth century was primarily a school of engineering, and Sherman and his fellow cadets spent more than two-thirds of their time on that subject, primarily under the tutelage of Professor Dennis Hart Mahan, West Point's leading scholar both in engineering and military science. Mahan, the author of numerous textbooks on civil and military engineering and military science, also provided the training these future officers received in the art of war. Mahan had much to say about entrenchments and defensive works of various sorts, but he was also an admirer of Napoleon, of that general's grand offensive movements and battles of annihilation.[10]

Had he not accumulated so many demerits, Sherman would have ranked higher within his class. One of his favorite illicit pastimes was the preparation of food in his quarters—strictly against regulations—and sharing it with fellow cadets in after-hours repasts. All such nonregulation food was known in cadet parlance as *hash,* and by his third year at West Point, Sherman, as fellow Ohio cadet William S. Rosecrans recalled, "was considered the best hash-maker at West Point"—adding that this distinction was "a great honor" among the cadets. Sometimes, he and his friends would cap a late-night feast with a clandestine visit to Benny Haven's tavern, two miles from the academy. The legendary inn was the favorite resort of two generations of West Point cadets in search of palatable food, strong drink, and raucous conviviality—and since it was strictly off-limits, it was also a source of numerous demerits for cadets caught frequenting it. And Sherman found plenty of ways to score demerits—keeping a messy room, talking in ranks, neglecting to salute a superior—to name a few. During his final year at the academy, his worst in deportment, he amassed one hundred forty-eight of the two hundred annual demerits that would have triggered his expulsion.[11]

Sherman was popular with his fellow cadets. Some of the acquaintances and friends gained at West Point would be men with whom Sherman would deal in one way or another for the rest of his life. Three classes ahead of him, North Carolinian Braxton Bragg was friendly with Sherman, and Massachusetts cadet Joseph Hooker was not. Handsome Pennsylvanian John C. Pemberton was also in the same class. New Yorker Henry W. Halleck, whose owlish face seemed appropriate for the studious habits that made him third in his class, and Marylander Edward O. C. Ord, Sherman's first roommate, were one year ahead of Sherman. The shy and mannerly Virginian, George H. Thomas was among Sherman's own classmates. Ulysses Simpson Grant, another Ohio cadet, arrived on campus at the beginning of Sherman's last year.[12]

As Sherman neared the end of his four years at West Point, the Ewings urged him to leave the army on graduation and pursue a civilian career, perhaps the law, but Sherman wanted to stay in the army and feared falling into continued dependence on Thomas Ewing. About that time, when Sherman got into a tight spot financially, he wrote not to Ewing but to his mother, Mary Sherman, requesting the loan of five dollars. "I do not wish ever to ask Mr. Ewing again for assistance," he explained. Determined to make his own way in the world, Sherman proceeded eagerly toward a military career.[13]

Graduation came on July 1, 1840. Of the ninety-four cadets who had entered the academy four years prior as part of Sherman's class, forty-two made it through to graduation. Of those, Sherman ranked sixth—and would have ranked fourth had it not been for all the demerits he had racked up. A fourth-place class rank would have put him in the elite corps of engineers. Sixth was good enough for artillery, the next best assignment. After the customary postgraduation furlough, Sherman reported late that summer, as ordered, to Governor's Island, New York, for transportation to Florida, where he was to take up his duties as a newly commissioned second lieutenant in Company A, Third U.S. Artillery Regiment.[14]

He joined his company at Fort Pierce, on the east coast of Florida about seventy miles below Cape Canaveral. There, he spent the next fifteen months in service that grew increasingly onerous and boring. The Second Seminole War was in progress, but it was a guerrilla conflict, in which the soldiers were rarely able to come to grips with the elusive Seminoles. Sherman played a minor role in negotiations with Seminole leader Coacoochee, but little came of the effort. The most interesting activity Sherman found was catching fish and turtles.[15]

In November 1841, he received a promotion to first lieutenant, a remarkably early advance for the army of that day, and Sherman may have had Thomas Ewing's favor to thank for it. With the promotion came a posting to Company G, Third Artillery Regiment, stationed near St. Augustine, Florida. There, Sherman commanded a twenty-man detachment, which guarded the one-family settlement of Picolata, eighteen miles from town. His tenure was uneventful, but the duty was better than at Fort Pierce. Mail came once a month and occasional visits to St. Augustine allowed him to enjoy the social life of that venerable town of three thousand inhabitants. He had been there only three months when in March 1842 the government decided that it had sufficiently suppressed the Seminoles.[16]

No longer needed in Florida, Company G next received orders to relocate to the Alabama coast for a three-month stint in Fort Morgan—and then to Fort Moultrie, outside Charleston, South Carolina. The latter post had gained its fame as a palmetto-log fortification that stood off British attack in 1776. In later years, the army had rebuilt it with masonry walls and two-story barracks inside. Outside the walls, the fashionable settlement of Moultrieville had grown up, composed of the airy seaside cottages where wealthy Charlestonians summered in the sea breezes. While much of the army's strength had been deployed against the Seminoles in Florida, Fort Moultrie, like Fort Morgan, had been unoccupied but now once again garrisoned and set in military order, the fort harbored four companies—B, D, and K, along with Sherman's G—as well as the band and headquarters of the Third Artillery.[17]

Military duties made few demands on a soldier's time at Fort Moultrie. Dress parade, guard mount, and inspection occupied the garrison until scarcely midmorning. Thereafter, Sherman wrote, "each one kills time to suit himself till reveille of next morning commences the new routine." The city of Charleston offered its diversions. Sherman was impressed with its architectural beauty and the dynamism of its bustling docks with their massive stockpiles of cotton and rice and the shouts and songs of the black stevedores. On the other hand, he and his fellow officers found the Charleston social scene tiresome. "Smirks, smiles, pride and vanity, hypocrisy and flippance reign triumphant," among the Charlestonians, Sherman wrote. He and his fellow officers, feeling that the army needed to be represented at social events in order to maintain community relations, were soon taking turns pulling social duty. To ease the boredom, Sherman resorted to painting pictures and writing letters. Sherman's most faithful correspondent was his foster sister, Ellen Ewing, who was four years his junior. [18]

In 1843, Sherman spent several months of furlough in Ohio, visiting family in Lancaster, Mansfield, and Columbus and helping his brothers arrange his mother's finances and living arrangements. His return journey to Charleston was by way of the Mississippi River. The Father of Waters fascinated Sherman, and he wrote with interest of its many sights, including the river towns of Memphis and Vicksburg. Early in 1844, the army assigned him to an investigation of claims that had been made by volunteer soldiers from the Seminole War for lost horses or equipment. The inquest, which lasted until the late spring of that year, was headquartered successively in Marietta and Augusta, Georgia, and in Bellefonte, Alabama. With his restless mind and abundant energy, Sherman spent all of his free time riding over the hills and valleys of North Georgia, sketching the terrain and admiring such features as Kennesaw Mountain. [19]

While back in Ohio the year before, he had made up his mind to marry his foster sister Ellen. By letter, he proposed to her and in another letter sought her father's approval. Both replies were favorable, but Ellen's came with conditions. She wanted him to get out of the army and take up a civilian occupation in Ohio. She would not, she wrote, consent to live at any substantial distance from Lancaster and her family. And she wanted him to become a practicing Catholic.

Sherman was unwilling on all counts. He felt he was unprepared for any career outside the army and was unwilling to go back and begin at the bottom of some new calling when he would need a regular steady income immediately if he was to marry. He believed the army was his only realistic chance for such an income, and he was determined to maintain his independence from his foster father and prospective father-in-law. He did not want to become a civilian, and if he did, he certainly did not want it to be in Ohio, least of all near Lancaster. As for Catholicism, Sherman said he wished to believe but could not quite do so. Over the next two years, earnest and somewhat pained letters made their way back and forth between Ohio and South Carolina.[20]

The crisis typified in many ways the tension of Sherman's childhood, youth, and young manhood. He owed much to the Ewings' generosity. They had taken him in, nurtured him, and secured his entrance into an honorable profession. Yet, he longed to make his own way, to stand on his own legs, and he dreaded a return to dependence on Thomas Ewing's generosity. The long-continued tension was intensified almost unbearably by Sherman's love for Ellen and her demand that he leave the only profession he felt offered him any hope of the independence he craved. Then, in the midst of this crisis, outside events intervened.

CHAPTER TWO

"A Dead Cock in the Pit,"
1846–1861

WHILE SHERMAN HAD BEEN AT WEST POINT, STUDYING, making hash, and sneaking off to Benny Haven's, while he had served as a young officer on various Southern posts and decided he wanted to marry his foster sister, events had been developing on the stage of national politics that would shape the path of his life over the next few years, and indirectly, mold the landscape of his career over the decades to follow.

In 1836, the year Sherman entered West Point, American settlers in the Mexican province of Tejas had thrown off the rule of the tyrant Antonio Lopez de Santa Anna and established themselves as the Republic of Texas. Mexico never admitted Texas's right to independence but failed in military efforts to reclaim the province. Texas sought annexation by the United States, but Congress held back—partially in fear that annexation would bring war with Mexico and partially from the belief in northern antislavery circles that the whole history of Texas had been little more than a plot to add more slave states to the Union.

In 1843, President John Tyler picked up the issue of Texas annexation in hopes of capitalizing politically both on the Southern passion to extend the realm of slavery and on the nationwide enthusiasm for Manifest Destiny. It was a powerful combination, but in the fickle ways of politics, it redounded not to his benefit but to that of presidential-contender James K. Polk, who announced in favor of annexing not only Texas but all the far-off Oregon country as well—new land for the South and new land for the North. Polk won the election, and before he could take office, Tyler pushed through a joint resolution annexing Texas during a final lame-duck session of Congress.[1] Mexico broke diplomatic relations and asserted its continued ownership of some of the territory claimed by Texas—and by now the United States. Polk sought to negotiate, but Mexico would not receive his emissary. Desiring to maintain U.S. claims, in 1846, Polk sent troops into the disputed zone, and Mexican troops attacked them, leading to the outbreak of war between the two countries.[2]

In far-off Charleston, Sherman fretted that he would be left out of the conflict. Active participation in the war in a far-off part of the country would prolong his separation from Ellen and delay his planned marriage to her, perhaps by several years. Yet as a professional officer he could not afford to sit out the war while his rivals gained distinction and promotion. He applied for transfer to the war zone but instead received an assignment to recruiting duty at Fort Columbus, New York. He tried every trick he could think of to get into the war, even accompanying a batch of recruits on their way to the fighting front. The effort got him no farther than Cincinnati, where he received a tongue lashing from a superior officer and unequivocal orders to get back to his post.[3]

In June 1846, Sherman received orders to report to Company F, Third Artillery, then in New York preparing to take ship for California via Cape Horn. These were not the orders Sherman wanted; he had hoped to join Zachary Taylor's army, which was preparing to advance into Mexico—but at least his new orders would take him to a minor theater of the war. Company F, Third Artillery would travel on the U.S. Navy sloop-of-war *Lexington,* with orders to cooperate with the navy in seizing Mexican outposts on either Monterey or San Francisco bays. Sherman felt eager for adventure and excited about being among the first in the new territory.[4]

On July 14, the *Lexington* set sail from New York, and Sherman was soon adapting to the monotonous rhythm of shipboard life. The officers read a great deal—none more so than the accompanying engineer officer, Sherman's West Point acquaintance, Henry W. Halleck, who had recently published a book entitled *Elements of Military Art and Science.* His fellow officers marveled at Halleck's single-minded studiousness during the voyage. All the while, the *Lexington* glided on at a stately pace, never exceeding 11.5 knots in the most favorable winds. In September, *Lexington* put in at Rio de Janeiro for a week. Even while he and his fellow officers continued to lament that they were missing the war, Sherman rhapsodized about the beauty of the harbor and its surrounding mountains and enjoyed its novel sights and exotic food. Back at sea, the army officers amused themselves near Cape Horn by catching some of the numerous albatrosses that swooped down to the deck to pick up scraps of food. The sailors, in the best Ancient Mariner tradition, blamed the landlubbers' poaching for the unusually heavy gales that buffeted *Lexington* for twenty-six days as she clawed her way around the cape with pitching decks and ice-rimed rigging. At last, on January 26, 1847, they finally arrived off Monterey, California. "Thank God," Sherman wrote, "after 198 days at Sea we have got here."[5]

Going ashore, Sherman and his fellow soldiers found that the fighting was over and settled down to occupation duty. Colonel Richard B. Mason, the commander, named Sherman his adjutant. There was little to relieve the monotony, and the always restless Sherman predictably grew bored and unhappy. He had much clerical work to do for Mason, and he complained of "bending over a table" all day. Worse, reports steadily trickled into California of the exploits of the army under Winfield Scott, including the other companies of the Third Artillery, as it fought its way into Mexico City. With all his colleagues winning recognition while he languished in this obscure place where it seemed nothing had ever happened or ever would, Sherman grew depressed.[6]

Late in the spring of 1848, a messenger arrived in Monterey from Sutter's Fort, the settlement of Swiss immigrant Johann Augustus Sutter, announcing the discovery of gold on the American River. Sutter had sent along a small sample of the ore, which Sherman tested as best he could with what he could recall from his West Point mineralogy class, and he concluded that it was indeed gold. That discovery did not particularly excite Sherman and Mason at the time. They considered it a minor curiosity.[7]

In fact, because of Sutter's discovery, people were soon flocking to the American River from all over California. New farms were left idle, houses vacant; soldiers deserted. Up the coast from Monterey one hundred twenty miles, the sleepy town of Yerba Buena, recently renamed San Francisco, became even sleepier as most of its male population departed for the gold fields. Sherman persuaded Mason that they needed to make a visit to the gold fields themselves so that they could send an eyewitness report to the government. Colonel, adjutant, and four soldiers set out from Monterey on June 17 and reached San Francisco three days later to find the town as nearly deserted as reports had claimed. Continuing up the bank of the Sacramento and then the American, they reached Sutter's Fort in time to enjoy a massive Fourth of July celebration Sutter had thrown for nearby settlers.[8]

The next day, the expedition continued up the American, pausing to examine the placer gold deposits and to talk with those working them. Mason and Sherman's detachment reached Sutter's Mill, the site of the original discovery fifty miles from Sutter's Fort, and also scouted some of the diggings in the hills on either side of the America

River Valley. Sherman reckoned that in the course of their reconnaissance they had seen four thousand men, and he further calculated that those men were extracting about fifty thousand dollars in gold every day. Back in Monterey, Sherman wrote the formal report that Mason sent to Washington, along with several gold specimens. His were the words, widely published and reprinted again and again, which officially announced to the world that gold had been discovered in California.[9]

Ironically, the gold rush threatened to impoverish Sherman and other army officers stationed in California. The abundance of gold created severe inflation, and the steady stream of gold-seekers entering the region drove prices even higher. The officers, with their salaries set by law, found their purchasing power dwindling rapidly. In desperation, Sherman, Mason, and another officer each put up five hundred dollars to set up a store at Coloma, near the gold fields, with a hired clerk, to sell supplies and equipment to the fortune-seekers there. The effort proved successful, and the officers quadrupled their investments within the few months that the store was in operation. It proved just enough to keep them afloat financially in the wildly inflationary economy of goldrush California.[10]

In the spring of 1849, General Persifer F. Smith arrived in California to take over command from Colonel Mason. Sherman, who had requested transfer to the East, found that his wish had been denied and that he would be staying on as Smith's adjutant. Sherman grew depressed at his situation—stuck in California, thousands of miles from home and the civilized world, and his career in ruins after having missed participation in Mexican War combat. The future offered no prospect but a life of loneliness and boredom on this wild frontier; he would stagnate in rank while his erstwhile comrades, now distinguished combat veterans (those who were still alive), advanced to higher rank. Hopeless as the prospect of making his way in the civilian world had seemed, a career in the army now seemed more hopeless still, and he contemplated resigning. "Self respect," he wrote, "compels me therefore to quit the Profession which in time of war and trouble I have failed to merit." General Smith talked him out of it, promising that he would soon assign him to carry dispatches to the East, giving him a welcome respite from the isolation of California.[11]

On January 2, 1850, Sherman embarked on the steamer *Oregon* for the voyage to Panama, across the isthmus to take passage on the steamer *Crescent City,* and thus, to the eastern United States. Sherman and his comrades caught no albatrosses, and seas were calm. The entire trip took only thirty days, a substantial improvement over the *Lexington*'s one hundred ninety-eight-day westbound journey.[12]

Arriving in Washington, Sherman delivered his dispatches to the War Department and received a six-month leave of absence, spending most of the time in Washington lobbying for promotion with the army's adjutant general but making no headway. While in Washington, Sherman called frequently on the Ewings, who were then staying at Blair House since Thomas was now in Zachary Taylor's cabinet. The reunion with Ellen was pleasant. The two had kept up their correspondence during Sherman's California sojourn. Ellen still wanted him to become a Catholic, leave the army, and take over management of her father's salt works at Chauncey, Ohio, forty miles from Lancaster. Sherman remained uninterested in religion and worried about dependence on Thomas Ewing. Nevertheless, he and Ellen agreed to wed on May 1, 1850. Tecumseh and Ellen honeymooned at Niagara Falls and were back in the national capital in time to attend the Fourth of July celebration, at which Zachary Taylor was taken ill. As an aide to the adjutant general, Sherman participated in the president's state funeral. Then, he was in the visitors' gallery of the Senate chamber several days later to see Taylor's vice president, Milliard Fillmore, take the oath of office as that nation's thirteenth president.[13]

These were exciting times to be in Washington. The debates over what would become the Compromise of 1850 were in full swing, and one could see history being made. The war with Mexico and the attendant acquisition of new lands had spawned controversy as to whether slavery should spread. When in 1850 California—populated almost overnight by the goldrush—applied for admission as a free state, the strife became intense. Southerners seethed with rage, threatening secession if their demands for the expansion of slavery were not met. To avert the showdown, the aged Henry Clay introduced compromise legislation calling for admission of California as a free state but in return making substantial concessions to proslavery interests. Debate raged throughout the summer and featured some of the most renowned orators in the history of the Senate making their greatest speeches. Sherman attended frequently, to listen to speeches by Daniel Webster and Henry Clay. He sat in the visitors' gallery, and once, thanks to his home-state senator, Thomas Corwin, at the back of the Senate floor itself. At last, in September, the compromise passed, and the slavery issue receded for a time.[14]

That fall, orders came for Sherman to join Company C, Third Artillery, at Jefferson Barracks, Missouri. Ellen was pregnant and at her parents' insistence remained with them in Lancaster, much to Sherman's dismay. Shortly after his arrival at Jefferson Barracks, he was promoted to commissary captain and stationed in nearby St. Louis. In his letters to Ellen, he praised St. Louis and wrote of his desire to have her there with him. Back in Lancaster, on January 28, 1851, Ellen delivered their first child, a daughter named Maria. In March, Sherman traveled to Lancaster and brought Ellen and baby Maria, nicknamed Minnie, back to St. Louis.[15]

They enjoyed a year together in St. Louis in a small house Sherman purchased, but Ellen grew more and more homesick for Lancaster while Sherman grew tired of his clerical job and began to pine for more adventure, even for the wild goldfields of California. In the summer of 1852, Ellen and Minnie went to stay with the Ewings in Lancaster while Sherman went on temporary duty to Kansas, but after his return to St. Louis, his family still remained in Lancaster, with Thomas Ewing writing to ask his permission for Ellen to stay longer. Grudgingly, Sherman agreed.[16]

His next posting was to New Orleans, where the army wanted him to straighten out corruption in the commissary department. He did, working energetically and maintaining rigid integrity. Yet, though he rented a house, Ellen still declined to join him. She was expecting another baby in November. The child, Mary Elizabeth, to be called Lizzie, was born November 17, and the following month Ellen and their two daughters joined Sherman in New Orleans. He was happy to have them, but Ellen demanded a more luxurious lifestyle than Sherman's army salary could support, and she kept up the familiar litany of reasons why he should leave the army.[17]

The same month that Ellen and the girls rejoined him in New Orleans, Sherman heard from Henry S. Turner, a friend who was a St. Louis banker. Turner was impressed with Sherman's experience as a commissary officer, and before that, as a quartermaster. He also noted that Sherman had done well in managing some of his father-in-law's property in St. Louis. Turner and his banking partner James H. Lucas planned to open a branch in San Francisco. Would Sherman like to head the new bank and draw an annual salary of four thousand dollars? He was not sure. He received only one thousand five hundred dollars per year in the army, but leaving was a big step. He also had to wonder if he could ever get Ellen to the West Coast. Still, it would satisfy her constant demand that he become a civilian. At the same time, it would provide a larger income and maintain his independence— and geographical distance—from Thomas Ewing. Sherman agreed.[18]

Sending Ellen and the girls back to Lancaster, he set out once again for California in the spring of 1853. He found San Francisco as untamed as he left it three years before but much bigger. The burgeoning city had by this time grown to contain some fifty thousand inhabitants, all of whom seemed to be making money rapidly and spending it with equal speed. Sherman was disturbed that Lucas and Turner had not provided sufficient capital for the bank. To persuade them to put up more, he took a ship around the Horn yet again and was back in Missouri by the middle of July. The partners met most of his demands. Preparing to set out for California yet again in September, Sherman insisted this time that his wife and daughters should accompany him. The Ewings objected. Sherman should go to California again and leave Ellen and the girls with them in Lancaster. Or, if not that, then Sherman should resign his bank job and come to work for Thomas Ewing in Ohio. When their son-in-law remained adamant, they shifted their demands and clamored to have the Shermans leave Minnie in Lancaster. Cump and Ellen acquiesced.[19]

Thus, leaving their oldest daughter as a sort of hostage to her grandparents, the Shermans journeyed to California, traveling by steamship and across the Isthmus of Panama. Back in San Francisco, Sherman purchased a brick house on Green Street and settled down to the business of banking. Ellen was not happy. In her letters, she complained incessantly of the flies, the fleas, the dust, the mud, the crowds, and San Francisco in general. She cried a great deal. Then, she became pregnant again, and everything got worse. When not fretting about her own situation in California, she worried about Minnie's health back in Ohio. Minnie had been in fine health when they left, and letters said she still was, but Ellen feared that the child would die before she got back. She complained constantly to Sherman that she would rather live in the meanest shack in Lancaster than the finest mansion in San Francisco, and she accused him of "making a poor exchange of friends for money." Meanwhile, letters from Thomas Ewing regularly offered comfortable employment in the Chauncey salt works, but Sherman staunchly maintained, "I would rather be at the head of the bank in San Francisco, a position I obtained by my own efforts."[20]

Sherman managed his bank well, displaying some of the qualities that would later make him a successful general. In 1855 the failure of a St. Louis bank, Page and Bacon, whose San Francisco branch was the largest in the city, set off a run on all the San Francisco banks. Seven of the city's nineteen banks failed, but Sherman's careful management of Lucas and Turner kept it standing solidly throughout the storm, meeting every depositor's demand with full payments in cash. Sherman personally was a tower of strength in the crisis, calmly encouraging depositors and fellow businessmen. When it was over, Ellen told him she wished his bank had failed, for then they would have gone back to Ohio.[21]

Sherman was a highly respected man in the community, and some of his friends wanted to run him for city treasurer. He was on the board of the first railroad in the state and was grand marshal of the parade celebrating the anniversary of California's statehood. He served for a time as commanding general of the California militia but resigned in frustration in 1856 when the local U.S. Army commander, Gen. John E. Wool, refused to provide the weapons he had promised Sherman so that his militia could combat a large vigilante organization.[22]

Late in 1856, Sherman's St. Louis partners, Lucas and Turner, decided to close the San Francisco branch. They were pleased with the job Sherman had done of running it, but in the volatile California economy, the branch had never been as profitable as they had hoped. In the place of the San Francisco branch, they planned to open a new branch in New York City and make Sherman its director. Sherman was flattered at their confidence but saddened that he had not succeeded in making the San Francisco branch pay as well as expected. He was also apprehensive about the highly competitive business environment in New York. Ellen was, of course, ecstatic at the prospect of being closer to Lancaster and her parents.[23]

It took six months to close out operations in San Francisco. Sherman was scrupulously honest. He had operated a fund, separate from the bank, to invest moneys entrusted to him by some of his army officer friends, and when he closed out California operations for the bank, he also closed the fund. In doing so, he went to the length of making good the investment losses of the officers, even though he bore no responsibility. As punctilious as his father, Sherman sold a number of parcels of his own land in California and Illinois until the officers who had trusted him had received their money, with interest, to the last penny.[24]

No sooner was the new branch up and running in New York than disaster hit in the form of the Panic of 1857. The crisis struck in

August of that year. Once again the banking world shook, and other banks crumbled. By his wise management Sherman was able to bring his bank through the storm as he had the San Francisco branch two years before. This time, however, doom overtook him from another quarter. The Panic of 1857 was a nationwide phenomenon, affecting St. Louis as well as New York. In October, the home bank of Lucas and Turner failed, dragging down Sherman's still solvent New York branch, and Sherman found himself unemployed.[25]

Bad times followed. Sherman tried several angles to get back into the army, but there were no openings. Passing through St. Louis about that time, he ran into an old West Point acquaintance, also now in civilian life and down on his luck. Ulysses Grant was in the process of failing to make a go of it on a small farm he called "Hard-scrabble," not far from St. Louis. It occurred to Sherman "that West Point and the regular army were not good schools for farmers [and] bankers." Finally, reduced to desperation Sherman faced his complete defeat as a man and accepted his father-in-law's standing offer of a job at the Chauncey salt works. In the end, it appeared, Ewing had won. Tecumseh was still his ward, still the helpless recipient of his charity.[26]

Late in July 1858, he arrived in Lancaster beaten and bitter, along with a delighted Ellen, five-year-old daughter Mary Elizabeth, called Lizzie, and four-year-old son William Ewing, whom the Sherman's called Willy. Sherman was slated to take over management of the salt works that fall, but trouble brewed almost immediately. Sherman's sister Elizabeth lived nearby, and she and Ellen fell to squabbling. Elizabeth blamed Ellen for undermining Tecumseh and bringing about his failure in business. Ellen found Elizabeth insufficiently respectful toward her devout Catholicism. Seizing the strife as his first escape opportunity, Sherman asked Thomas Ewing if he could move to Leavenworth, Kansas, to join his brothers-in-law Thomas Jr. and Boyle Ewing in their combination law and property management business there. Ewing agreed, and Sherman set off. Ellen and the children remained in Lancaster.[27]

Arriving in Kansas late in 1858, Sherman worked in property management, tending Ewing's various assets in the area. On the side, he did whatever else he could to make a few dollars—bought and sold horses and mules or corn and potatoes—hoping somehow to scrape the money together to allow him to buy a house so that he could bring Ellen and the children out from Ohio. But there was never enough.

During the winter of 1858 and 1859, he was able to borrow a house from Thomas Ewing, Jr., who was away for the season. Ellen arrived with the children in November, and soon thereafter, she was boasting in letters that she no longer felt homesick. She had been in Kansas scarcely three months before she was once again pregnant and longing for Lancaster, goaded by letters from her father urging her to come back. In the spring of 1859, Sherman had to give up the house, and his family went back to Ohio. Meanwhile, nothing he did seemed to prosper. "I look upon myself as a dead cock in the pit," he wrote, "not worthy of further notice."[28]

Then, an old army friend, Don Carlos Buell, mentioned that he had heard that the new Louisiana Military Seminary in Alexandria, Louisiana, was looking for a superintendent and offered to recommend Sherman. After assuring themselves that Sherman, though an Ohioan, was no abolitionist, the directors hired him. Arriving in Alexandria in the fall of 1859, Sherman found that the seminary boasted an imposing new building, devoid of furniture, in the midst of a dense pine woods three miles from town. He immediately got busy purchasing books and equipment and working with the board of directors to lay out the rules and regulations of the new institution, patterned in many ways after West Point and the Virginia Military Institute. He got along well with his new slaveholding neighbors. Sherman expressed his approval of slavery and his condemnation of abolitionists and made clear that he was not the ideological twin of his younger brother John, by then a prominent Republican member of Congress.[29]

The school officially opened its doors on January 2, 1860 to an initial class of nineteen students, some of them as young as fifteen.

Other students joined the class during the months that followed. Though strict and demanding, Sherman was popular with the cadets, occasionally regaling them with tales of his life in the army or in California. He was more content and at peace in his new role than he had been with any lot that had fallen to him since leaving the army.[30]

By the time the first school year came to an end on July 31, 1860, the presidential campaign of that year was in full swing and had taken some unusual turns. The Republicans had nominated Abraham Lincoln on a platform of preventing the spread of slavery to new territories. The Democratic Party had split between one faction that favored letting white settlers in new territories decide the status of slavery there, and another that loudly demanded active federal protection of slavery in every territory. The former nominated Senator Stephen A. Douglas of Illinois, and the latter nominated Vice President John C. Breckinridge of Kentucky. The Whig Party had disintegrated several years before, its antislavery elements migrating to the Republicans and its strong proslavery elements to the Democrats. Moderate proslavery Whigs organized the Constitutional Union Party and nominated John Bell of Tennessee as its presidential candidate. Many Southern leaders threatened loudly that their states would secede from the Union if Lincoln or any "Black Republican" won the election.

As far as Sherman was concerned, the two sides were contending over abstractions. They should mind their own business and forget such matters as the moral rights and wrongs of slavery. Secession, however, was treason, and if the South took that step, Sherman let it be known that he would support the federal government in suppressing it by force.[31]

Lincoln won the election. In December came word that South Carolina had seceded. Sherman wept at the news. In the days that followed, he lamented to his Louisiana friends, "You are driving me and hundreds of others out of the South, who have cast fortunes here, love your people and want to stay." When news arrived several days later that the Louisiana militia, acting on the governor's orders, had taken over two U.S. forts on the Mississippi, Sherman tendered his resignation. The seminary board begged him to stay, and he agreed to remain at least for the present. Then, on January 10, 1861, the militia seized the U.S. arsenal at Baton Rouge. The rebellious state forces shipped more than two thousand of the arsenal's weapons for storage at the seminary, under Sherman's direct command. That was too much. Sadly, on January 18, he wrote his letter of resignation to the governor. He stayed in Alexandria for another month, tying up loose ends at the school and making sure he had fulfilled all his duties. Then, on February 19, at a special formation of the cadets, he bade an emotional farewell and set out for New Orleans to take passage on a northbound train.[32]

CHAPTER THREE

Failure, 1861–1862

ARRIVING IN LANCASTER, SHERMAN FOUND WAITING FOR
him a letter from his brother John inviting him to come to Washington to discuss the present troubled state of the country. Another letter
was from Lucas and Turner, offering him a position as president of the
Fifth Street Railroad Company of St. Louis. The offer interested Sherman, but he decided to visit Washington first.[1]

In the capital city in early March, his brother, the congressman,
took him to see the president. "Mr. President, this is my brother,
Colonel Sherman, who is just up from Louisiana," explained John.
"He may give you some information you want."

"Ah!" Lincoln replied, "How are they getting along down there?"

"They think they are getting along swimmingly," Tecumseh
growled. "They are preparing for war."

"Oh well!" quipped Lincoln. "I guess we'll manage to keep
house."

Tecumseh misinterpreted the president's reply as ignorant and unconcerned. In fact, Lincoln had at least as clear a view of the gravity of the situation at that moment as did the recently arrived visitor from Louisiana, but the president saw no value in magnifying the crisis. Sherman was outraged and pricked in his pride that Lincoln had not reacted with more alarm to what he considered an alarming revelation. Alone with his brother once again after leaving the White House, Tecumseh growled that the politicians had gotten the country into its present mess, and he would leave them to get out as best they could.[2]

Sherman went back to Lancaster and announced to Ellen that he was taking the job with the Fifth Street Railroad Company of St. Louis. On March 20, he arrived in St. Louis with his family in tow. The Shermans now had five children—Minnie, whom the Ewings had finally returned, Lizzie, and Willie, as well as Thomas Ewing "Tommy" Sherman, born in San Francisco in 1856, and Eleanor Mary "Elly" Sherman, born two years later. Ellen was pregnant again. Sherman went right to work on the railroad, putting in long days at the office. It was soon running smoothly and profitably. His home life was neither smooth nor profitable but certainly ran along familiar tracks. Ellen spent money far beyond Sherman's means and complained incessantly of homesickness.[3]

Then came Fort Sumter. Located in the harbor of Charleston, South Carolina, Sumter, along with its one hundred twenty-seven-man U.S. Army garrison, had become an important symbol to both sides. If Lincoln removed the garrison, he would be admitting Confederate independence. If Confederate president Jefferson Davis allowed it to stay, he would be admitting continued U.S. sovereignty, despite the fact that the garrison was doing nothing at all. When Lincoln moved to resupply the fort, Davis ordered his forces to attack. Early on the morning of April 12, Confederate guns opened fire and the fort's commander, Major Robert Anderson, surrendered on the afternoon of the following day. As the Constitution provided in such cases, Lincoln called on the states for seventy-five thousand volunteers to put down the insurrection. The North responded enthusiastically, but the slave states of Virginia, North Carolina, Tennessee, and Arkansas announced their own secession and joined the Confederacy.

In May, Sherman wrote to Secretary of War Simon Cameron offering his military services. Before he could receive an answer, events in St. Louis brought the war much closer to home. The prosecession state militia had recently been counterbalanced by a Unionist home guard, composed largely of antislavery German immigrants. Secessionist and Unionist citizen-soldiers eyed each other with suspicion. The trigger for open fighting was a number of crates of weapons from the Baton Rouge arsenal. The same weapons that had chased Sherman out of Alexandria had, as it were, dogged his steps to Missouri. Jefferson Davis sent the firearms to the secessionist Missouri militia under false pretenses, since Missouri did not claim to be part of the Confederacy. Detecting the clandestine shipment, the commander of U.S. forces in Missouri, Brigadier General Nathaniel Lyon, also received information that the secessionists planned to use the added firepower to capture the U.S. arsenal in St. Louis. Rather than wait until he was cornered in the arsenal, Lyon used his loyal German-American home guards, with a small leavening of regulars, to surround the secessionist encampment and capture the would-be attackers.[4]

As Lyon's troops marched their prisoners through the streets of St. Louis on their way to incarceration, crowds gathered. Some bystanders, including Sherman and his son Willy, were simply curious. Others were proslavery and were armed and seething with rage. One of them shot a German-American officer with his revolver. The soldiers fired back, and pandemonium broke loose. Sherman grabbed Willy and dived into a ditch, covering the lad with his body. When the smoke finally cleared, twenty-eight were dead and numerous others wounded.[5]

A few days later, on May 14, Sherman received notice that he had been appointed colonel of the newly organized Thirteenth U.S. Infantry Regiment, and by June 11, he was in the national capital. Military affairs were in rapid flux, and before the end of the month, Sherman had moved up to command the Third Brigade of Brigadier

General Daniel Tyler's First Division, part of the field army Brigadier General Irvin McDowell was putting together in preparation to march on Richmond.[6]

Three of the four regiments in Sherman's new brigade were composed of volunteers, and they had almost as many doubts about him as he did about them. Soldiers in those days had distinct ideas of what they wanted their officers to look like—generally a sort of Currier and Ives version of Napoleon crossing the Alps—and Sherman did not measure up. His uniform, when he bothered to wear a uniform, was old and ill fitting, his appearance gangly and disheveled. Under a broad-brimmed straw hat, he looked more agrarian than martial, but he obviously knew what he was doing, and as he had the cadets in Louisiana, he charmed the men with his tales of western adventure. He also drilled them incessantly and yelled at them until he was hoarse.[7]

While he worked hard to whip his raw recruits into shape, Sherman worried about the attitude of the country at large. Newspapers, such as Horace Greeley's influential *New York Tribune,* talked as if the Union army had only to march forward and the Southern rabble would disperse. This annoyingly inconvenient war would then be over, and none too soon, most Americans seemed to think. Sherman knew from his experience with Southerners that they were bitterly determined to achieve the independence of their slaveholders' republic. Sherman believed the war would be long and hard and would shed far more blood than most Americans then realized, and he worried about the nation's will to see it through.

Sherman had been in his new command scarcely two weeks when, in response to the "On to Richmond" clamor of the press, Lincoln directed McDowell to advance. "It is true that you are green," he reasoned with the reluctant general, "but they are green also; you are all green together." That was true, for what it was worth, but Lincoln was calling on McDowell's army to perform an offensive maneuver, a much more challenging task for green troops than merely standing on the defensive, as the opposing Confederate army of General P. G. T. Beauregard would be doing.

On July 15, the army left its camps around Washington and marched west toward Centreville, Virginia, about twenty-five miles away, on a road that would, if all went well, take them to Richmond, the new capital of the Confederacy, a little more than one hundred miles to the south. The march was just the sort of disorderly proceeding that Sherman had feared from undisciplined volunteers. Many fell out of ranks to rest, sightsee or forage—that is, confiscate food from civilians. Foraging was allowed by the laws and customs of war, but when it was carried on in such a disorganized manner, it tended to weaken and demoralize the army. Also, Federal authorities were still trying to woo the South back into the Union. They were pursuing a conciliatory policy, and consequently, it was often expedient to treat Southerners as friendly rather than enemy civilians—not as appropriate targets for foraging. Sherman strove to suppress foraging in his command. Catching Private Alpheus T. Budlong of the Second Wisconsin with a quarter of freshly butchered local mutton, Sherman had the meat confiscated and the man arrested. He was unmoved by Budlong's excuse: "I was hungry, and it was rebel mutton anyhow."[8]

On July 18 Sherman and his brigade were in a supporting role when Tyler, exceeding his orders from McDowell, led the division's lead brigade into an unsuccessful skirmish at Blackburn's Ford, a strongly-held Confederate position on a stream called Bull Run. Sherman moved up near the end of the short fight to cover the retreat. He later remembered it as "the first time in my life I saw cannonballs strike men and crash through the trees and saplings above and around us, and realized the always sickening confusion as one approaches a fight from the rear."[9]

McDowell planned his assault for the morning of Sunday, July 21. Tyler's division would threaten a frontal attack while another Union column turned the Rebel flank. Sherman's position was near a stone bridge where the Warrenton Turnpike crossed Bull Run. His assignment was to look threatening until the flanking assault on the other side of the creek got rolling. Then, as soon as the Confederates pulled away from the crossing to meet that threat, he was to take his brigade across the creek and join the assault.[10]

As scheduled, the men of Tyler's division rolled out of their blankets in their camps outside Centreville at 2:00 A.M. on the morning of July 21, and at 3:00 A.M., moved out for Bull Run, Sherman's brigade second in the column. The march was slow and tedious. Sherman would later recall "standing for hours wondering what was meant." The road passed between dense woods that shut out the light of the moon and the early dawn. "You could not see your hand before your face," a soldier recalled. Colonel Robert C. Schenck's brigade had the lead. Nervous about the possibility of an ambush, Schenck proceeded slowly, tentatively, with frequent halts, while Schenck's skirmishers stumbled through the gloomy woods on either side of the road ahead of the column. "We had to feel our way," one of them remembered.[11]

The sun rose just after 5:00 A.M., and another half hour passed before the division was across the rickety bridge over Cub Run, one-half mile from its camps. Schenck continued his cautious advance until Tyler decided they had reached the place to deploy. Schenck's brigade filed to the left of the road, Sherman's to the right in a wooded area. Then, the line moved forward to the crest of a gentle ridge where the woods gave way to an open field sloping down toward Bull Run in front of them. At 6:00 A.M., Tyler ordered one of his artillery batteries to fire the three successive shots that would signal the flanking column that his force was in place and ready to begin its demonstration against the Confederate center.[12]

The operation proceeded as planned. The Union flanking column, thirteen-thousand men in two divisions, got across Bull Run undetected and struck the Rebel flank, which quickly buckled. To meet the new threat, the Rebels desperately shifted troops, including those guarding Bull Run near the Stone Bridge. Yet, Tyler was slow to follow. Eager to advance, Sherman found the wait tedious.

At 11:00 A.M., an order arrived from McDowell directing Tyler to "press forward his attack." Tyler ordered Sherman to take his brigade and find a crossing of the creek somewhere upstream from the bridge. While waiting in the woods that morning, Sherman had scouted along the skirmish line, finding out as much as he could about the situation in front. About 9:00 A.M., he had seen a couple of Confederate horsemen ride along a hill on the opposite side of the valley, then down to the stream and across it at a ford. The Rebels rode a short distance toward the Union troops, and one of them brandished his weapon over his head and shouted curses at the "black Abolitionists," as he called them. Then, the Confederates turned and rode back to the Confederate side of Bull Run, having showed Sherman the location of a convenient ford.[13]

Receiving Tyler's order, Sherman moved aggressively to cross the stream. He had his men drop their blankets and haversacks and then march at the double-quick. They splashed through the ford, and Sherman led them up the steep bank toward Matthews Hill, where several Confederate brigades had been fighting a desperate struggle against the Union flanking column. Rebel resistance was just giving way on Matthews Hill, partially in response to the sight of Sherman's threat to the Confederate flank. Sherman's men, approaching from the right-rear of the Confederates who had been defending the hill, encountered some of the retreating graycoats, and Sherman's Sixty-ninth New York exchanged volleys with the Fourth Alabama. The Sixty-ninth's Lieutenant Colonel Haggerty was shot dead before Sherman's eyes.

Continuing its advance, the brigade began to move over ground strewn with dead and wounded men and horses. That was a sobering sight for these unbloodied soldiers, but they sensed that their side was winning the battle, and they felt jubilant. Linking up with the flanking column, Sherman reported his position to McDowell. The Union commander was ebullient, and his staff officers and several subordinates were riding along their lines with shouts of "Victory!" "They are running!" and "The day is ours!" Only a final Rebel fallback line on Henry House Hill now stood between the victorious Federals and a position squarely in rear of Beauregard's army. McDowell ordered Sherman to set out at once in pursuit of the retreating Confederates.[14]

Offensive tactics presented an almost insoluble problem for Civil War generals. How to adapt the lines and columns of traditional infantry maneuvers to the new and more lethal environment on Civil War battlefields, which was created by improved weapons, was a question that never received a satisfactory answer during the conflict. The problem was made more difficult by less than expert troops trying to move across less than ideal terrain. In this first battle of the war, these difficulties were compounded by the inexperience of the officers, including Sherman, at commanding large bodies of troops. McDowell threw his forces at the Rebels a brigade or two at a time, and Sherman, whose previous largest command had been less than a hundred men, made matters worse by sending his regiments into action one at a time.

After advancing his brigade as far as the Sudley Road, Sherman had his troops take shelter there, where the road grade—eroded by wind, water, and wagons over its dirt surface—was sunken enough to provide a modicum of protection for prone infantrymen. McDowell moved other troops forward, and the fight for Henry House Hill got underway. Union troops surged up the hill again and again, but the Confederate defenders drove them back.[15]

Ordered to join the attack, Sherman sent his regiments forward one at a time, and one by one, they were repulsed. One of the attacks at first seemed successful, but fresh Confederates soon drove Sherman's troops back. The Rebels swept over Henry House Hill, driving Sherman's men and other Union troops before them. With that, and the failure of the additional flanking movement McDowell had ordered at the same time he sent Sherman forward, the Union army had shot its bolt and was capable of no further offensive action for the time being. McDowell decided to order his troops to pull back to their camps around Centreville, where they could take cover within an entrenched position and regroup overnight. The Union troops were exhausted and shaken, nearly untrained, and in some cases, poorly led. As the army fell back, it began to lose cohesion.

Sherman somehow did not receive the order to retreat, and his first indication of it came when he noticed that most of the rest of the army had already pulled back from Henry House Hill and that a battalion of Regulars, the rear guard of the entire army, was slowly falling back toward him, formed in square to repulse an expected Confederate cavalry pursuit. Sherman also noted with dismay that some of his men were setting out for the rear on their own. Forming his brigade into a square that he later had to admit was "irregular," he began to withdraw, but his men were not Regulars, and their formation disintegrated almost immediately—the men heading for the rear in a confused swarm, not panicked but largely disorganized.[16]

To make matters worse, numerous civilians, including several members of Congress, had come out from Washington to watch the battle—from what they had judged to be a safe distance. As the retreat began, the civilians hastily repacked their picnic baskets, jumped into their buggies and carriages, and headed for the rear, clogging the roads, impeding the soldiers' retreat, and providing the final ingredient needed to create full-scale confusion and panic in many of the army's units. Troops threw away their weapons and equipment and ran—despite all that McDowell, Sherman, and other officers could do to stop them.

Sherman somehow got the four regiments of his brigade back to the field near Centreville where they had encamped the night before. He drew them up in line and had them lie down to rest. Then, he lay down under a tree and fell asleep. He had not slept long when Tyler came and awakened him. McDowell had changed his orders. Too many of the troops were continuing their stampede right past Centreville and back up the road toward Washington—as if the Devil himself were after them, when, as far as Sherman could see, not even the Rebels were in pursuit. Nonetheless, with so much of the army stampeded, it would be dangerous for the rest to attempt to make a stand at Centreville, and for this reason, McDowell's new orders were to continue the retreat all the way back to Washington.[17]

Sherman awakened his aides, and together they got the brigade up and on the road. By that time it was about midnight. Sherman and his officers tried to keep the regiments together as units, but it was hopeless. His men were soon part of the undifferentiated horde of soldiers making their way toward Washington. Sherman and those traveling with him reached the brigade's former camps near Fort Corcoran around noon on July 22.[18]

The army was in an appalling state of confusion and indiscipline. Many of the soldiers were separated from their units and seemed uneager to rejoin them; they milled around instead, a partially-armed mob intent on working its way northward, into and perhaps through Washington itself. Sherman immediately took what steps he could to improve the situation. He ordered a local ferryman to stop conveying stragglers across to the north bank of the river, and he recommended to the adjutant general in Washington the placing of guards on all the bridges.[19]

In the days that followed, Sherman worked almost incessantly to try to reorganize his brigade and make it battle-worthy again. It was no easy task. Morale was abysmal, the men uninterested in further soldiering. Sherman denounced one group as "a pack of New York loafers and thieves" and got catcalls in return. The Sixty-ninth New York was a special problem. Its members believed their ninety-day enlistments should be reckoned from the time of their initial enlistment back in New York, but the authorities held that the ninety days started when the troops had signed the regimental muster book in Washington, several weeks later. As a consequence, the New Yorkers, mostly Irishmen, had asserted even before the battle that their time was up and they were entitled to go home. Persuaded to remain in the ranks for the "On to Richmond" push, they now wanted to go home more than ever.

Five days after the battle, a captain of the Sixty-ninth, in the presence of a crowd of enlisted men, airily announced to Sherman that he was going to New York that day. "I do not remember to have signed a leave for you," Sherman replied. The captain replied that he needed no leave. His enlistment was up, and he planned to go back to New York and return to his law practice. Many of the enlisted men had gathered around them, eagerly listening to see if the captain would get away with his bold intention. "Captain," Sherman said evenly, "this question of your term of service has been submitted to the rightful authority, and the decision has been published in orders. You are a soldier, and must submit to orders till you are properly discharged. If you attempt to leave without orders, it will be mutiny, and I will shoot you like a dog." Since Sherman had been standing with his hand rather ominously out of sight inside his overcoat, the captain decided not to test him.[20]

Later that day, Lincoln came to visit the camps, along with Secretary of War William H. Seward. Joining Lincoln in his carriage, Sherman asked the president to "discourage all cheering," since it tended to create disorder among the troops. "No more hurrahing," Sherman urged. "No more humbug." Lincoln obliged. At the camp of each regiment of the brigade, when he stood to address the men, he urged calmness. "Don't cheer, boys," the president admonished, "I confess I rather like it myself, but Colonel Sherman here says it is not military; and I guess we better defer to his opinion." Then Lincoln would make a short speech, encouraging the men. Sherman had prided himself on his disdain of politicians, especially Lincoln, but now he was impressed. He had listened to the nation's finest orators during the compromise debates in 1850, but he allowed that he had "never heard a man who spoke to the hearts of his hearers, as Mr. Lincoln spoke to our soldiers that day."[21]

The best was yet to come. When they reached the camp of the Sixty-ninth New York, the mutiny-minded captain stepped boldly up to Lincoln. "Mr. President," he said, "I have a cause of grievance. This morning I went to speak to Colonel Sherman, and he threatened to shoot me." "Threatened to shoot you?" said Lincoln. "Yes, sir, he threatened to shoot me." Lincoln paused, looked at the officer, then at Sherman. Then leaning over toward the officer from where he sat in his carriage, the president said in a stage whisper, audible for some distance, "Well, if I were you, and he threatened to shoot, I would not trust him, for I believe he would do it." The officer slunk away amid roars of laughter from the soldiers crowding around. Sherman's opinion of Lincoln rose dramatically.[22]

Gradually, military affairs in northern Virginia settled into a routine. New regiments, who had enlisted for three years, arrived from the North and replaced the ninety-day regiments. Sherman drilled his troops diligently, working hard to bone up on the manuals that would bring him up to date on the development of tactics during the decade he had been out of the army. In mid-August, somewhat to his surprise, he received a promotion to brigadier general. His brigade had done as well as any at Bull Run, and professionally trained officers were at a premium as the nation vastly expanded its army.

Some days later, he received a note from Robert Anderson, his old commanding officer of Fort Moultrie days. Anderson, more recently the hero of Fort Sumter, was now a brigadier general senior to Sherman. He requested Sherman to pay him a visit at his room at Willard's Hotel in Washington. As a native Kentuckian, Anderson was the choice of the Lincoln administration to command Union forces in that crucial state, now teetering in the balance between secession and the Union. Anderson's orders placed him in command of the Department of the Cumberland and said he could choose four brigadier generals from the forces around Washington to go to Kentucky with him as his lieutenants. Two of those who first came to Anderson's mind were men who had last served under him with the rank of lieutenant—former Third Artillery members Tecumseh Sherman and George H. Thomas, both now brigadier generals. Sherman was happy at the prospect of going west. When Lincoln met with Anderson and the officers slated for transfer to Kentucky, Sherman emphasized that he did not want the responsibility of overall command but was willing to go as a subordinate of Anderson. Lincoln laughed and said that would be no problem. His difficulty was finding places for all the generals who did want to hold top commands.[23]

They reached Kentucky in early September. General Albert Sidney Johnston commanded Confederate troops there, and though his force was not large, Anderson's was not much larger. Johnston assumed an aggressive posture that was unnerving to his opponent. Anderson put Sherman in command of all the available troops around Louisville and had him advance twenty-six miles toward Bowling Green on the Louisville and Nashville Railroad, guarding against a rumored advance by Johnston that turned out to be nothing but another of the wily Rebel's many feints. In the days that followed, newly raised Midwestern regiments trickled into Louisville, and Anderson forwarded them to Sherman, who soon had two full brigades at Elizabethtown, ready to march on Bowling Green if ordered.[24]

Early October brought disturbing news from Anderson. The Hero of Fort Sumter was fifty-six years old and in poor health. The stress of commanding a department had worn him down to the point that by the beginning of October he badly needed a long rest. On October 6, Anderson turned the command over to Sherman, who was next in rank within the department. Sherman still wanted to avoid the top command in Kentucky and wrote to Washington asking to be relieved. He received a promise that Brigadier General Don Carlos Buell was on his way from California, and when Buell arrived, he would supersede Sherman in command of the Department of the Cumberland.[25]

Like Anderson before him, Sherman was taken in by Johnston's feigned aggressiveness. Knowing the weakness of his own forces, Sherman assumed Johnston knew it too, and—oblivious to Confederate weakness—Sherman could not understand why Johnston did not attack. He thought that the Rebels could have marched into Louisville any time Johnston chose to do so—something Sherman would still be asserting more than a decade later. He felt the administration did not understand the danger on his front and was sending troops and first-rate weapons to other sectors while neglecting his. Additionally, dispatches from Washington suggested that he was overestimating his opponent's numbers, which was true, and that he should soon take the offensive and advance into East Tennessee, an idea Sherman considered stark madness. The situation played on

Sherman's emotions, and years later he admitted, "Conscious of our weakness, I was unnecessarily unhappy, and doubtless exhibited it too much to those near me."[26]

He certainly did. To Ellen he wrote letters of unrelieved gloom. To Ulysses S. Grant, commanding the district of the Department of Missouri that bordered Sherman's own Department of the Cumberland, he wrote expressing his fears of being overrun. To Secretary of the Treasury Salmon P. Chase, he wrote to say that he hoped he would be adequately supported with supplies. To Abraham Lincoln, he wrote complaining of his inadequate manpower and resources and urging the administration to do more for his department. He concluded the letter with a one-word imperative sentence: "Answer." He followed up that letter with additional letters to the president to the same effect.[27]

Around the middle of October, Secretary of War Simon Cameron passed through Louisville on his way back to Washington after a visit to St. Louis. Sherman importuned the secretary to meet with him so that he could explain the needs of the Department of the Cumberland. Their conference took place in Sherman's quarters in the Galt House Hotel. Several newspaper reporters were traveling with Cameron, and the secretary insisted that they remain for the discussion. Sherman reluctantly described what he believed was the weakness and vulnerability of his department. He asserted that it would take sixty-thousand men to defend his area and two-hundred thousand men for him to go on the offensive and drive the Rebels all the way to the Gulf of Mexico. The secretary of war was aghast. Such numbers were undreamed of at the time, although this estimate would later prove prescient. Sherman felt the meeting had been a success. Before leaving, Cameron promised to send reinforcements.[28]

Back in the capital, Cameron characterized Sherman's request for two-hundred thousand men as "insane." Newspapers quickly picked up the story, and Sherman was appalled to find in the *New York Tribune* a complete account of his conference with Cameron. Worse, Sherman could soon read in any number of journals that he was "crazy, insane, and mad." Meanwhile, Assistant Secretary of War Thomas W. Scott voiced the suspicions of many when he said, "Sherman's gone in the head, he's luny." Considering the situation from his headquarters in Washington, General-in-chief George B. McClellan, dispatched Colonel Thomas M. Key to Louisville to report on Sherman's condition. After several days at Sherman's headquarters, Key telegraphed McClellan that Sherman was approaching a nervous collapse.[29]

The colonel was right. Sherman had been under intense stress since taking command of his brigade before Bull Run. Since the battle, he been working almost around the clock, frequently neglecting to go to bed at all, pushing himself day after day. In Louisville, he got into the habit of waiting in the telegraph office until 3:00 A.M., looking for incoming messages, then pacing the hotel corridor outside his room for the rest of the night. A human begin simply could not continue indefinitely without sleep, running on nothing but nerves. It was common in the Civil War for department commanders to overestimate their enemies, think they were outnumbered, and plead that their departments needed reinforcing more than all others, but Sherman's constant extreme statements had their source in his state of nearly frantic despair and utter exhaustion.[30]

Fortunately, Don Carlos Buell arrived in Louisville on November 13 to take over command of the Department of the Cumberland. Sherman's new orders directed him to report to Major General Henry W. Halleck, who had replaced Major General John C. Frémont as command of the Department of Missouri. Relieved to be relieved from the Kentucky command, Sherman nevertheless remained depressed, contemplating suicide. Tipped off by a staff officer, Ellen Sherman decided to come to Louisville to see her husband. She took his brother, Ohio Senator John Sherman, with her. They found Tecumseh withdrawn. John told his brother that he was "laboring under some strange illusions," and Cump warned John that the Rebels were about to launch a "simultaneous attack on St. Louis, Louisville, and Cincinnati."[31]

Halleck assigned Sherman to inspect Union positions around Sedalia, Missouri. Rumors of Sherman's insanity continued. Although his specific military advice was good, some of Sherman's dispatches suggested that he once again apprehended a massive Rebel attack. Ellen again came to see him, traveling as far as St. Louis. Halleck recalled Sherman from Sedalia to meet her and had Sherman assessed by departmental medical director J. B. Wright, who concluded that Sherman was in a condition "of such nervousness that he was unfit for command." Finally, at the urging of his wife, his staff, and his commander, Sherman requested a twenty-day leave of absence and set off back to Lancaster with Ellen. Halleck, reporting on the matter to McClellan, wrote, "I am satisfied that General S[herman]'s physical and mental system is so completely broken by labor and care as to render him for the present entirely unfit for duty. Perhaps a few weeks rest will restore him. I am satisfied that in his present condition it would be dangerous to give him a command here."[32]

Back in Lancaster, away from the stress of command, Sherman rested, and his nerves returned to normal. He continued to be distressed, however, over what he was reading in the newspapers. A December 11 headline in the *Cincinnati Commercial* proclaimed, "General William T. Sherman Insane," and *Frank Leslie's Illustrated Newspaper* commented, "General Sherman, who lately commanded in Kentucky, is said to be insane. It is charitable to think so." There was a great deal more, much of it untrue or at best wildly exaggerated. Sherman had long harbored intense dislike of newsmen. They had, he thought, contributed to the public panics that had made his banking career difficult. In the current conflict they had published information that was of use to the enemy, and now, he believed, they were trying to destroy him—and doing a good job of it. Sherman had never been reticent in expressing his opinion of newspapermen, and many of them no doubt saw the present situation as an opportunity to chastise one of their critics.[33]

Rest was all Sherman had needed, however, and his mental state was soon back to normal. When he returned from leave, on December 23, Halleck cautiously assigned him to safe duty commanding the camp of instruction at Benton Barracks, outside St. Louis. He was to prepare the new regiments for service in the field and assess the competence of their volunteer officers. All went smoothly during the nearly two months of his command. Sherman proved a good teacher, and the recruits and their equally green officers learned their new business rapidly.[34]

On February 13, Halleck ordered Sherman to turn over Benton Barracks to his second-in-command and take command at Paducah, Kentucky. Located where the Tennessee River joined the Ohio, Paducah was at that time an important base for Grant's advance up the Tennessee River. One week before, Grant, with the aid of a squadron of river gunboats commanded by Flag Officer Andrew H. Foote, had captured the Rebel stronghold of Fort Henry, seventy-five miles above Paducah and just inside the state of Tennessee. At the moment Grant was engaged in a battle for Fort Donelson, located on the Cumberland River a dozen miles from Fort Henry. One of Halleck's first orders to Sherman at his new post was a February 15 telegram directing him to "send General Grant every thing you can spare from Paducah."[35]

The next day, Fort Donelson surrendered. Grant's twin victories were the first major turning point of the war. Union forces had ripped open the defenses of the Confederacy's heartland. Rebel forces would have to evacuate Kentucky. Half of Tennessee was at the Federals' mercy, and the rest, along with Mississippi and Alabama, lay open to Union invasion.

For Sherman, the transfer to Paducah meant a move closer to the fighting front and one that would have him performing a role of direct support to the armies then battling the Rebels, but it still kept him out of a direct combat command. Halleck was easing Sherman toward a more responsible position but was not ready to expose him to the kind of pressure that had led to his previous breakdown. He had yet to live down the past, and the shadow of his previous failure still hung over him. In the weeks to come he would find a second chance.

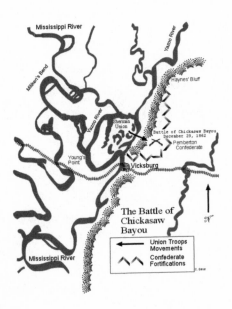

Mississippi River

Milliken's Bend

Yazoo River

Haynes' Bluff

Sherman
Union

Battle of Chickasaw Bayou
December 29, 1862

Pemberton
Confederate

Young's
Point

Vicksburg

Mississippi River

The Battle of
Chickasaw
Bayou

← Union Troops
   Movements

⋀⋀ Confederate
   Fortifications

C. Gear

𝒩

CHAPTER FOUR

From Paducah to
Chickasaw Bayou, 1862

HALLECK PLANNED TO BEGIN REAPING THE FRUITS OF Grant's February victories by sending Grant's army up the Tennessee River to seize the rail junction town of Corinth, Mississippi, about twenty miles from the river, just south of the Tennessee-Mississippi line. For the offensive against Corinth, Halleck, who had recently been promoted to command of all of the Union armies west of the Appalachians, planned to bring together not only Grant's army but also Buell's, which had just reached Nashville, and Brigadier General John Pope's small army, which had recently operated along the Mississippi with the navy. With all three armies united on the Tennessee River not far from Corinth, Halleck would leave his headquarters in St. Louis to join them in the field and lead the combined force in the march on Corinth.

Sherman's role in this was at first to push steamboats, troops, and supplies up the various rivers to the commands that needed them. Then, in early March, Halleck gave him command of a division newly organized at Paducah and ordered him to join the expedition up the Tennessee. Sherman's regiments were green. Most had had their weapons less than two weeks. One, the Fifty-third Ohio, received its rifles the day it boarded the steamboat for the trip up river. The division caught up with the Army of the Tennessee on March 9, and with it, moved upstream to Savannah, Tennessee, a hamlet on the east bank thirty miles from Corinth.[1]

On March 14, General C. F. Smith, temporarily commanding the army in place of Grant, ordered Sherman to take his division in its transports, escorted by two of the navy's gunboats, up the river nearly to Eastport, Mississippi—thirty-five miles from Savannah and thirty miles east of Corinth—proceed inland, and break the Memphis and Charleston Railroad east of Corinth. The Memphis and Charleston was the most important railroad in the Confederacy; it was the South's only continuous east-west rail line and a vital strategic link between the two main theaters of fighting. On the way up river, the division passed a steamboat landing on the west bank, about ten miles above Savannah. The naval commander told Sherman the place was called Pittsburg Landing and was the main landing serving Corinth, twenty miles to the south-southwest. The gunboats had driven off a few Rebels there some days prior. Sherman sent word to Smith that Union troops ought to seize Pittsburg Landing as soon as possible.[2]

Continuing upriver, they found a promising landing site about two miles below Eastport. A road led southwestward about twenty miles to the hamlet of Burnsville, on the Memphis and Charleston about fifteen miles east of Corinth. Because breaking the railroad there would fulfill Smith's orders perfectly, Sherman sent the cavalry on ahead to wreck the railroad—with the infantry and artillery to follow in support. Unfortunately, shortly after the division landed, a day of intermittent rain gave way to a night of torrential downpour. Flooded streams made the march impossible and inundated river bottoms nearly prevented reembarking. As it was, the last half-mile to the landing was so deep the boatmen shuttled the infantry over in yawls, while the artillerists fastened long ropes to their guns and dragged them across, under water.[3]

Taking his sodden division back down river, Sherman found General Stephen Hurlbut's division in steamboats moored at Pittsburg Landing. Leaving his own division there, Sherman continued the ten miles to Savannah and reported to Smith, who ordered him to disembark his division and that of Hurlbut, his junior, at Pittsburg Landing. Both should then move far enough from the river to leave room for the rest of the army to encamp there. In a few days, Smith planned to join them and lead an expedition to break the Memphis and Charleston.[4]

In obedience to Smith's orders, Sherman disembarked and marched his division three miles from the river along the main Corinth Road, arranging his camps along a low ridge. Two of his brigades straddled the Corinth Road, their flanks meeting near a Methodist meetinghouse, known as Shiloh Church. A third brigade continued the line farther to the right, covering the Purdy Road. Sherman's lines faced generally south-southwest, and his regimental camps were arranged so that when each regiment stood on its color line, the division was more or less in line of battle. During the next few days, more troops arrived. Benjamin Prentiss's brand-new division camped on Sherman's right. John McClernand's, William Wallace's, and Hurlbut's divisions all encamped to the rear, between Sherman's camps and the landing.[5]

On March 17, Grant resumed command of the army, but like Smith, kept his headquarters at Savannah in order to make early contact with Don Carlos Buell's Army of the Ohio, marching overland from Nashville on Halleck's orders. Halleck had an inadequate appreciation of the value of time in warfare; Buell had none at all. His plodding march left the Army of the Tennessee sitting idly at Pittsburg Landing for three weeks.[6]

Halleck warned repeatedly that Grant must do nothing that might bring on a clash with the Rebels. In Halleck's mind, this warning would prevent the unnervingly aggressive Grant from taking any more of the risks that Halleck dreaded—or any more laurels he coveted for himself—but the policy came at a price. Enemy cavalry normally lurked just beyond the army's fringes, scouting its activities and preventing its learning the enemy's whereabouts, numbers, and intentions. The only way a general could "see" beyond this screen was to push the enemy cavalry out of the way, but that entailed fighting, which Halleck had forbidden. The difficulty of this inability to see the enemy's main force fell directly on Sherman. With Grant downstream at Savannah, Sherman was the senior officer at the encampment and also the only West Point graduate among the division commanders. His camps were on the outer perimeter, and Grant trusted him to detect the approach of the enemy.[7]

Halleck's orders denied Sherman the means of doing so. On April 3, one of Sherman's brigades made a training march five miles out on the Corinth Road before encountering Confederate cavalry. Since Sherman's orders were "not to be drawn into battle," the brigade commander retreated without pressing forward to find out what might be behind the Confederate horsemen. The following evening near sunset, Confederate cavalry hit one of Sherman's picket outposts, capturing several men. Sherman's division and the rest of the encampment were soon under arms, and Sherman led one of his brigades several miles in pursuit of the retreating raiders until they encountered Confederate artillery. Again, following orders to avoid battle, Sherman fell back.[8]

Though Halleck's orders prevented him gaining adequate information about what lay beyond his lines, Sherman grossly misinterpreted the information he did have—and then disregarded all evidence that did not fit the interpretation he had chosen. In Kentucky six months before, Sherman had suffered disgrace for overestimating the size and aggressiveness of the Confederate forces he faced. Determined not to make the same mistake again, he stubbornly clung to the belief that the main Rebel army—including all but a regiment or two of its infantry—was no closer than Corinth and was most emphatically not going to approach Pittsburg Landing much less attack the Army of the Tennessee. What his men had been encountering on almost a daily basis recently was nothing more than cavalry, backed up as usual by a battery of horse artillery. The real fight, he maintained, would not take place until they advanced on Corinth.[9]

On the morning of April 4, several men of Sherman's division patrolled forward through woods fronting the open fields where the division was encamped. At the far edge of the woods, they came to another large clearing and saw, several hundred yards away, extensive Confederate camps including infantry and artillery. A sergeant returned to camp with the report, and several minutes later Sherman's response came back: the sergeant was to be placed under arrest "for bringing a false report into camp."[10]

Next morning, April 5, Sherman's pickets engaged in continuous long-range sharpshooting with Rebel horsemen. Yet, in a dispatch to Grant, Sherman wrote, "I have no doubt that nothing will occur today more than some picket firing. The enemy is saucy, but got the worst of it yesterday, and will not press our pickets far." He concluded, "I do not apprehend anything like an attack on our position."[11]

That afternoon as Sherman's division drilled in a large field in front of its lines, a number of his soldiers sighted horsemen in what appeared to be butternut uniforms watching the proceedings from the far end of the field. At the conclusion of the drill, Colonel Jesse Appler, commanding Sherman's extreme left-flank regiment, the Fifty-third Ohio, sent a platoon to that end of the field to investigate the suspicious riders. Some minutes later the platoon leader returned and reported that the horseman had fallen back at his approach but that when he pursued he had run into a heavy Confederate skirmish line. That was enough for Appler. He ordered the drummer to beat the long roll summoning the Fifty-third into line of battle, and he dispatched a staff officer to report to division headquarters. The regiment was waiting in line when the officer returned. "Colonel Appler," he said in a voice loud enough for the men to hear, "General Sherman says: Take your d——d regiment back to Ohio. There is no enemy nearer than Corinth." Appler's troops laughed, and did not wait for orders to break ranks and go back to boiling their coffee.[12]

That evening, Sherman sent a circular to his brigade commanders explaining the latest intelligence on the Confederate forces lurking beyond their lines. The Rebels, Sherman announced, consisted of two regiments of cavalry, two of infantry, and a battery of artillery. Later that evening, Sherman dined with Benjamin Prentiss, commander of the other frontline division, whose troops had been bringing in the same sort of reports of enemy activity. The volunteer general was worried, but Sherman remained confident that next morning a single brigade would easily dismiss the pesky Rebels. That night, Appler stationed a sixteen-man picket at the far end of the long clearing, near where the Rebels had lurked that afternoon. Farther to the right, on the picket line in front of the center of Sherman's division, Sergeant Ed Gordon tried counting the number of campfires he could see in front of his post and finally gave up. Neither Appler nor Gordon sent notice to Sherman. By that time, it was clear that such reports were not welcome at division headquarters.[13]

Sunday, April 6, Sherman awoke to the sound of "a good deal of picket firing." Not thinking it especially urgent, he took his breakfast as usual. A staff officer of the Fifty-third Ohio brought word from Appler that he had heard firing and was putting his regiment into line of battle. Sherman quipped, "You must be badly scared over there." Nor did he let it disturb him, when drummers in the camps of his two nearest brigades beat the long roll. After breakfast, the volume and persistence of firing, coupled with further messages from his subordinates, drew Sherman out to survey the situation. By the time he and his staff mounted up, his subordinates already had the division in line of battle.[14]

From the rising ground on which his headquarters were located, Sherman could see the length of a long clearing called Rea Field, past Appler's camp, to the far end where troops appeared to be crossing the field, as though marching toward Prentiss's flank, out of sight in the woods beyond.[15]

Trailed by his staff, Sherman galloped along the line of his right brigade, reaching the camp of the Fifty-third just before 7:00 A.M. He rode along the front of the regiment's line, reined his horse, and peered at the troops crossing the other end of the field, several hundred yards away. As he gazed through field glasses, a line of Rebel soldiers emerged from the underbrush fringing Shiloh Creek, about a hundred yards to his right, leveling their rifles in his direction. "General," shouted an officer of the Fifty-third, "look to your right." Sherman lowered the glasses and glanced right. "My God, we are attacked!" he blurted, instinctively raising one hand, as if to ward off a blow.

The Confederates volleyed. One bullet hit the hand Sherman had raised, inflicting a minor wound. Another struck Sherman's orderly squarely in the head, and the soldier toppled to the ground dead. Spurring his horse back to where Appler stood, Sherman shouted, "Hold your position. I will support you." Then he galloped back toward the center of his line.[16]

Like a general in any era, Sherman had had to sort through conflicting data in the days and hours leading up to the battle of Shiloh. As any general can, he succumbed to the temptation of assuming his enemy would act in the way he wanted the enemy to act, and interpreted all evidence to mean only that. He stubbornly shoehorned every reported fact into his theory and discarded any report that could not be made to fit at all. The sudden Rebel attack had shown him to be horribly mistaken. Such a blunder might have been fatal to the career of a general, even one as well connected as Sherman was. That it was not, was largely a factor of how Sherman performed a few hours later.

By the time he had galloped his horse the several hundred yards back to Shiloh Church, his entire line was hotly engaged. Energetically but calmly and without a trace of panic, Sherman made sure his troops were deployed correctly—fighting well, responding appropriately to Confederate movements, and receiving ammunition resupply as needed. The intense stimulation of battle seemed exactly what Sherman's overactive mind needed, and he seemed to become calmer while combat raged around him. With a makeshift bandage on his wounded hand, he rode along his lines, encouraging his inexperienced troops by his resolute example. One soldier described him "erect in his saddle . . . a veritable war eagle." Another recalled, "I remember how glad we were to see General Sherman, with a rag on his hand, ride along our lines."[17]

Sherman's position was a good one, and his men repulsed one Rebel attack after another. As they did, their sector attracted additional Confederate strength. A half-mile gap separated Sherman's left in Rea Field from Prentiss's right in the woods to the east. Gray-clad attackers exploited the gap, and shortly before 9:00 A.M. Prentiss's division collapsed. Confederate commanding general Albert Sidney Johnston, believing he had severed the Federals from the river, shifted most of his strength to Sherman's sector, eager to trap the Army of the Tennessee against Snake Creek's impenetrable swamps. Meanwhile, in the Confederate rear, Johnston's second-in-command, P. G. T. Beauregard, dispatched reserves toward the sound of the heaviest firing—straight into Sherman's sector.

The added weight finally became too much for Sherman's division. Appler's Fifty-third Ohio, exposed on the flank, crumbled first, though not before nearly wiping out a Mississippi regiment that had attacked it. Then the rest of the division began to unravel from left to right. Around 10:00 A.M., Sherman ordered it to fall back to the line of the Hamburg-Purdy Road, several hundred yards to the rear. As Sherman's troops took up the new position, McClernand's division moved up and came into line on their left, finally filling the gap in the Union front. Unlike Sherman's men, McClernand's were combat veterans, having fought at Fort Donelson. They were also fresh, whereas Sherman's division had already fought for more than three hours. Thus manned, the new line looked strong.[18]

About this time, Grant reached Sherman's sector. The Army of the Tennessee commander had been in Savannah that morning when he heard the sound of cannon, boarded a steamboat kept ready there, and raced up river to join his army. After visiting other portions of the line, he stopped to see how Sherman was doing. An aide to Grant later recalled Sherman's appearance when they reached him. "Sherman's stock had become pulled around until the part that should have been in the front rested under one of his ears, while his whole appearance indicated hard and earnest work."

By that time Sherman had had two horses shot under him, and a glancing bullet had bruised his shoulder. Grant expressed "great satisfaction" with Sherman's performance. Hastily, he briefed his division commander on the battle in other sectors. "Things did not look as well over on the left," Grant explained, but he had sent for Lew Wallace's division to come down from Crump's Landing, and it should be on hand soon, he hoped, as a much needed reinforcement. Then, Grant and his staff hurried off toward other parts of the field. "I never deemed it important to stay long with Sherman," Grant later wrote.[19]

The stand along the Hamburg-Purdy Road proved surprisingly short-lived. In part, this was because most of the weight of Johnston's army was still bearing down on this sector, giving the Rebels an overwhelming advantage in numbers. In part, it was because McClernand, who was an amateur general, lacked an eye for terrain and how to use it in battle. Placing his line on the precise crest rather than the forward slope of a gentle ridge just behind the road, McClernand put his men at a severe disadvantage against the more numerous Confederates swarming toward them. McClernand's men were fully exposed to enemy fire, while the Rebels could take shelter behind the curve of the ground in a shallow swale in front of the ridge. His line took heavy casualties and collapsed within minutes.

When McClernand's line broke, Sherman's division, which was itself under very heavy pressure, had to fall back again, but Sherman was not content to yield the ground so easily. Halting his troops about five hundred yards in the rear of the Hamburg-Purdy Road, he regrouped and then, around noon, went over to the offensive. With what was left of McClernand's division advancing on his left, Sherman launched a counterattack. Thanks in part to the fact that his right brigade extended somewhat beyond the Rebel flank, the attack met with initial success. The Confederate lines crumpled, and for a few minutes, the flow of the battle was reversed, and Sherman's Federals were chasing the fleeing graycoats.

Superior numbers finally asserted themselves. Johnston had brought to the battlefield an army slightly larger than the Union force at Pittsburg Landing. More than two thirds of that Confederate army was now massed against Sherman and McClernand's divisions. Against that weight of numbers, their attack ground to a halt. Sherman's right brigade had veered left in pursuit of the retreating Confederates, and now the Rebels surged back and flanked it in turn, sending it back in retreat. Once again under heavy pressure from the front, the rest of Sherman's division and McClernand's fell back to the point from which they had launched their counterattack. Their effort had not been wasted however. They had won vital time and had kept the Confederates fighting chiefly on their front instead of massing troops where they could have done more damage elsewhere on the field.[20]

By the middle of the afternoon, the intensity of the fighting had waned slightly on Sherman's front, though it continued to be strong enough to force him to draw back somewhat farther late in the day. To the left of Sherman's division, the rest of the Army of the Tennessee, or what was left of it, held a line that curved all the way back to a point on the river a few hundred yards below Pittsburg Landing. From this final defensive line, Grant beat off the last attacks of the day. Even as night fell and the firing ceased, the first units of Buell's Army of the Ohio were arriving on the opposite bank of the Tennessee and being ferried across by steamboat. The day's fighting, and with it the Army of the Tennessee's dire situation, were at last over.

Like nearly all the other officers within the Union perimeter around Pittsburg Landing that night, Sherman assumed the next order of business would be the army's withdrawal, putting the Tennessee River between itself and the victorious Rebels. With his division secure and the day's fighting over, Sherman went to look up Grant and see how his commander planned to handle the withdrawal. That night was miserable. Heavy thunderstorms rolled over the Tennessee Valley, blotting out moon and stars and dumping torrents of cold rain on the weary soldiers and the suffering wounded. Grant's headquarters boat was full of wounded and the ghastly scenes of surgeons plying their bone saws. So too was the cabin at the landing that he had for a time used as headquarters earlier that day. Sherman finally found him standing under a tree, lantern in one hand, cigar clamped in his teeth. "Well, Grant," said Sherman, "we've had the devil's own day, haven't we."

"Yes," Grant replied. "Lick 'em tomorrow, though."[21]

In fact, Grant had no thought of retreating. Reinforced by Major General Lew Wallace's division, just arrived from Crump's Landing, and three divisions of Buell's army, he went over to the offensive at first light on the morning of April 7, driving the Rebels back across the ground of the previous day's fighting. The combat did not match the previous day's sustained fury, but in the vicinity of a thicket near the Hamburg-Purdy Road, the fighting was so intense that Sherman would years later recall the musketry there as the heaviest he had heard during the war. Late in the day, his division recaptured its camps, riddled with bullets and ransacked by the Rebels. By that time the Confederate army had had enough and withdrew. Grant's army was in no condition for immediate pursuit.

The next day, April 8, Sherman led a limited pursuit with two of his brigades. They tangled briefly with Rebel cavalry under Brigadier General Nathan Bedford Forrest, driving off the gray-clad horsemen but proceeding no farther. Sherman saw abundant evidence that the Confederates were in full retreat, leaving behind much equipment and many of their wounded. The clash with Forrest, which occurred at a place known as Fallen Timbers, was the final action of what would be known as the Battle of Shiloh.[22]

Sherman's reputation rose sharply after Shiloh. That might have seemed strange, considering how completely he had allowed the enemy to surprise him, but his performance once battle was joined had been outstanding enough to blot out his failures in the preceding days. He had shown himself fearless under fire and unflappable in directing troops in the heat of battle. The men in the ranks were impressed, and so were Halleck and Grant. A few weeks after the battle, Sherman was promoted to major general of volunteers.[23]

The battle had the opposite impact on Grant's reputation. The loss of life had been out of proportion to anything the country had experienced before. More Americans died at Shiloh than in all the battles of all the nation's previous wars put together. Someone must be blamed, people assumed, and the newspaper editors picked Grant. Wildly-inaccurate stories told of the army being surprised so completely that soldiers were bayoneted in their tents—and all because Grant was drunk. None of it was true, but it was influential enough with the public that some believed Grant would have been the victim of mob violence had he appeared on the streets of some northern cities during the weeks after the battle.[24]

Grant could have tried to shift the blame to Sherman, on whom he had depended to provide intelligence from the front, but he never did. In fact, he refused to make any public defense of himself. Sherman repaid Grant's loyalty. When the lieutenant governor of Ohio published a harsh attack on Grant, Sherman replied with a letter, published in the *Cincinnati Commercial*, strongly defending Grant. The politician replied in another published letter, and Sherman rejoined with another of his own. He could do little, however, to defend Grant against their superior, Henry Halleck.[25]

Halleck arrived at Pittsburg Landing a few days after the battle. His hostility to Grant, suppressed by Lincoln's intervention the month before, now returned in the bureaucratic subtlety of which Halleck was master. Now that Buell's Army of the Ohio, and John Pope's Army of the Mississippi had joined the Army of the Tennessee at Pittsburg Landing, Halleck reorganized the combined force, making Grant second-in-command of the whole— with no duties. He then placed Sherman's old classmate, George H. Thomas, in command of what had been Grant's army and proceeded to belittle Grant in every way possible. For Grant, it was death by a thousand bureaucratic cuts and personal snubs. Since Halleck felt—mistakenly—that he dared not simply sack Grant, even in the wake of Shiloh, he hoped to drive him to resign his commission, and he nearly succeeded.[26]

While Halleck waged his campaign to rid himself of Grant, he also directed his combined force, some one-hundred thousand men, in a more or less equally gradual and cautious campaign against his other enemy, P. G. T. Beauregard, who had succeeded to command of the Rebel army when Johnston fell at Shiloh. Though he outnumbered Beauregard two-to-one, Halleck conducted the campaign as if he expected the enemy at any moment to fall on him in overwhelming strength. His average daily advance was twelve-hundred yards, and he had his men build elaborate entrenchments at the end of each day's increment. Beauregard, with his smaller numbers, could not attack Halleck or think of any other way to halt the Federals' inexorable progress toward Corinth. After six weeks, Halleck had reached the outskirts of the town, and Beauregard skillfully evacuated his army, leaving Halleck to take possession the next day of a relatively empty prize. The rail junction was his, but the Rebel army that had defended it had escaped to fight another day. Both sides were disappointed with the outcome of the campaign.

Shortly thereafter, Sherman paid a call on Halleck in his camps. In the course of conversation Halleck mentioned that Grant was leaving. Sherman asked why, and Halleck said he did not know but that Grant had asked for and received a thirty-day leave. On his way back to his own camp, Sherman stopped by to see Grant. He found him sorting and filing papers, while his staff packed up headquarters files. After the usual pleasantries Sherman asked if it was true that Grant was leaving. Grant said it was. Sherman asked why. "Sherman," Grant said, "you know. You know that I am in the way here. I have stood it as long as I can, and can endure it no longer." Where was Grant going? "St. Louis." Did he have any business there? "Not a bit."

Sherman knew that if Grant left now, on these terms, he would probably never return to active duty. He urged Grant to stay, citing his own case as an example. Before Shiloh, he had nearly been ruined by the newspapers saying he was crazy. Shiloh had restored his fortunes, and now he was "in high feather." If Grant left the army, the war would go right on without him. If he stayed, something might happen to restore his standing in the army. Besides, he would be just as unhappy sitting at home. Grant appreciated Sherman's advice and agreed not to leave without letting him know. Sherman was not the only one who urged Grant to stay, and Grant had other reasons for reconsidering his decision. Nevertheless, to the extent that Sherman's friendship contributed to saving for the Union the services of the man who was to prove its most able general, the episode should rate among Sherman's most significant contributions to victory.[27]

In the days that followed, Halleck dispersed the giant army with which he had taken Corinth—one division would remain at Corinth and the others would move to a West Tennessee or northern Mississippi whistle-stop, thereby allowing Halleck to focus on occupying the territory he had taken. Thomas went back to Buell's army, which Halleck sent east to threaten Chattanooga, albeit very slowly.

Sherman spent the first half of the summer trying to keep the railroad running and Confederate cavalry raiders away from it. It was a well-nigh impossible task, during which Sherman suffered from malaria and for the only time during the war had to ride in an ambulance while supervising his troops. In mid-July, Lincoln made Halleck general-in-chief of all Union armies, with headquarters in Washington. The command of Halleck's old department fell to Grant, and the command of Grant's former District of West Tennessee to Sherman, who moved his headquarters to Memphis. There Sherman drilled his troops, had fortifications built, kept order in the city, and promoted a restoration of commerce—while at the same time trying to prevent illegal trade with the enemy downriver.

Like generals occupying hostile territory in other wars, Sherman had to deal with guerrillas who struck at his forces from within the shelter of the civilian population. He tried to suppress straggling and pillaging by his own troops and extended aid to needy civilians, but he could be hard when he felt it necessary, applying pressure to the civilian population that harbored the guerrillas. When unarmed steamboats suffered random sniping, Sherman retaliated by having nearby settlements along the river burned or by expelling secessionist families from

Memphis. "We are not going to chase through the canebrakes and swamps the individuals who did the deeds," he wrote to a Tennessee civilian who appealed to him, "but will visit punishment upon the adherents of that cause which employs such agents." Grant approved.[28]

While Sherman administered Memphis, the late-summer and fall campaigns played out inconclusively. Dissatisfied with the lack of aggressiveness in his generals and lack of progress in the war as a whole, in October Lincoln replaced Buell with Major General William S. Rosecrans and gave John McClernand vague orders to lead a semi-independent expedition within Grant's department, down the Mississippi to take Vicksburg the most direct way possible. Grant received only bits and pieces of information about the behind-the-scenes scheming by which McClernand had won the assignment, but he quickly gathered that Washington wanted more aggressive action. He was only too happy to comply, since Halleck's disapproval of offensive operations had been all that was holding him back.

In mid-November, Grant and Sherman met at Columbus, Kentucky, to confer on their next move. Grant revealed that he was making plans to advance in Mississippi, now defended by Confederate John Pemberton, with an army on the south bank of the Tallahatchie. Grant wanted Sherman to advance with his command, now swelled by new regiments arriving from the North to some three divisions, and join him on the Tallahatchie for the showdown with Pemberton. As ordered, Sherman linked up with Grant's right on December 2, but the showdown never took place. Scouts revealed that Pemberton had abandoned the south bank of the Tallahatchie and fallen back fifty miles to the Yalobusha River near Grenada.[29]

During the march, Sherman dealt with the age-old and still current question of how much destruction to visit on the enemy population. His answer was that the property of enemy civilians should be completely at the mercy of the need to prosecute the war but not of the wanton cruelty of vandals in the ranks. When Confederate troops burned the bridge over the Tallahatchie at Wyatt, Sherman had his men dismantle a number of houses to use as materials for building a new bridge. When the residents remonstrated, Sherman insisted, "That bridge must be built if it takes the last house in the town." When they sought financial reimbursement, he referred them to the Confederate forces. "You let them burn the old bridge," he explained, "and I was forced to build another. To do this I was forced to use your houses, in exchange for which I give to you the bridge. Take good care of it; do not force me to build another."[30]

On the other hand, when Sherman came upon a group of his soldiers who had seized a fine carriage and four splendid horses from a planter and were riding down the road in luxury, he ordered them to dismount at once. One of the soldiers refused, at which Sherman flew into a rage, snatched a rifle from a nearby soldier and would have shot the man had the weapon been loaded. Once the men were all off the carriage, he had them unhitch the horses, get into the harness themselves, and pull the carriage the two miles back to its owner's house.[31]

On December 8, Sherman conferred with Grant in Oxford. Grant's easy success and lengthening supply lines prompted him to modify his original plan. He now proposed to send Sherman back to Memphis with one division. There, Sherman would gather up additional new troops steadily arriving from the North in response to Lincoln's mid-summer call for three-hundred thousand more volunteers. Thus reinforced, Sherman would take an army of about forty-thousand men down the Mississippi by steamboat, enter the Yazoo River just above Vicksburg, disembark, ascend the bluffs on the southeast side of the Yazoo onto the interior plateau of Mississippi, and enter Vicksburg through the back door—from the east, rather than via direct assault up the bluffs on which the town sat. Meanwhile, Grant would keep Pemberton occupied in the interior of Mississippi.[32]

Sherman arrived in Memphis on December 13 and one week later set out on the voyage down the river, escorted by a naval flotilla under Rear Admiral David Dixon Porter. On Christmas Day, Sherman's army disembarked on the south bank of the Yazoo. For the next three days, his men skirmished with Rebel forces, advancing through leafless woods draped in Spanish moss. By December 28, it was clear that their path through the bottomland along the Yazoo was cut off by a sluggish watercourse called Chickasaw Bayou. In fact, all the lowlands in this Delta country were laced with bayous—twisting, branching, and interlocking. Too small for gunboats, too large for easy fording by infantry, they were the bane of all efforts to get at Vicksburg.[33]

Troops could cross Chickasaw Bayou at two places, only one of which offered hope of a successful attack. Sherman assigned Major General A. J. Smith's division to make a feint at the less promising crossing and Major General George W. Morgan's to make the main assault at the other. Morgan was confident of success. "General," he told Sherman, "within ten minutes after you give the signal I'll be on those hills," indicating the bluffs on the far side of the bayou. He expressed the same confidence to other officers as well.[34]

On December 29, Sherman launched the assault. As expected, Smith's advance got nowhere. Morgan badly bungled his part, misdirecting his brigades and those of Frederick Steele's division, which was supporting him. The assault was a dismal failure, costing some one thousand seven hundred seventy-six casualties while causing less than two hundred Confederate casualties. It was an open question whether success would have been possible had Morgan not blundered. The Confederate position was almost impregnable. So great was the terrain advantage for the defenders that, despite the presence of some thirty-two thousand men in Sherman's command, Pemberton hardly needed all of the fourteen-thousand or so men he had along the line of the Walnut Hills, overlooking the bottomlands of Chickasaw Bayou and the Yazoo River.[35]

After this setback, Sherman thought for a time of having Steele's division storm Haynes's Bluff, farther up the Yazoo. The prospect was not encouraging, and the troops told off for the attack weighed their chances grimly. Then, shortly before daybreak on December 31, as the boats prepared to make their way up the Yazoo, fog made the movement impossible—much to the relief of Steele's soldiers. On the heels of the fog came heavy rain. Contemplating tree trunks with high-water marks ten feet above his soldiers' heads, Sherman decided it was time to go. During the night spanning January 1 and January 2 he reembarked his army.[36]

The next morning, McClernand arrived at the mouth of the Yazoo, and Sherman went aboard his boat to confer with him. McClernand announced that he had direct orders from Lincoln to take command of the Mississippi River expedition. He also informed Sherman that Grant had retreated to Memphis after Confederate cavalry had destroyed his supply depot at Holly Springs. Nothing more could be done against Vicksburg now, since Pemberton would be free to reinforce it from his army in the middle of the state. This left McClernand entirely at a loss, since his only plan—with which he had cajoled Lincoln into giving him this assignment outside proper channels—was a less sophisticated version of what Sherman had just attempted: go to Vicksburg and attack it. For the moment McClernand's only orders were that the troop-laden transports should assemble at Milliken's Bend, ten miles up river, and that the army should be reorganized into two corps, one commanded by Morgan and the other by Sherman.

Some days earlier the Union mail steamboat *Blue Wing* had been captured between Memphis and Milliken's Bend by a Rebel boat venturing out of the Arkansas River. That boat was based at Fort Hindman, a Confederate stronghold located at a bend of the river called Arkansas Post. A Rebel garrison of several thousand men was said to be there, and Sherman believed Union supply lines for any future efforts against Vicksburg would never be secure so long as Arkansas Post remained in Confederate hands. So, on January 4, he asked McClernand for permission to take his corps up the river and deal with the place. McClernand was skeptical, so Sherman suggested they meet with Porter and get his opinion. By this time, it was late at night, and going aboard the flagship, they had to disturb the admiral's sleep. Porter took an immediate dislike to McClernand and was further annoyed by the political general's supercilious manner toward Sherman. The admiral became so belligerent toward McClernand that Sherman finally asked to talk with him privately and urged him to set aside his personal feelings. Porter agreed, and when the pair rejoined McClernand all three soon came to agreement for the move against Arkansas Post. McClernand decided to go along and take his whole army.

They reached the vicinity of Arkansas Post and disembarked on January 10, spending the rest of the day skirmishing and closing in on the Rebel fortifications. During the night, Sherman made a personal reconnaissance in which he crept close to the enemy entrenchments, and hiding behind a stump, listened to the sounds of the Confederates preparing for the coming battle. He could almost make out their voices talking, and about 4:00 A.M. he listened as a Confederate bugler "sounded as pretty a reveille" as he had ever heard.[37]

By 10:00 that morning, January 11, all was ready. When the gunboats advanced and engaged the fort, the Union infantry advanced as well, using cover and keeping up a deadly fire to force the Confederates to keep their heads down. Rebel morale wilted under the pounding of Porter's heavy cannon and the inexorable approach of the Union foot soldiers. As the Federals prepared for the final rush to the parapet, white flags appeared along the Confederate line. The victory at Arkansas Post more than evened the score of the preceding week's loss. Against Union losses of one thousand forty-seven, McClernand's army had killed or captured virtually the entire Confederate garrison of about five thousand five hundred men.

Having destroyed the fort, the army headed back down the Arkansas in a snow storm and reached the Mississippi River. There, Grant met them. Nothing in McClernand's orders exempted him from Grant's authority as department commander, and Grant did not approve of the movement against Arkansas Post. From the vague reports he had heard in Memphis, it sounded like a wild goose chase. Sherman and Porter took him aside and explained that the movement had sound strategic reasons, and that seemed to mollify him. He ordered McClernand to take the army back down the Mississippi to the west bank just above Vicksburg. Morgan's corps, soon to be McClernand's own, encamped at Milliken's Bend. To Sherman's troops fell the honor of taking the encampments nearest Vicksburg. On January 22, Sherman went ashore with his men at Young's Point.[38]

The Vicksburg Campaign

- - - Union Troops
      Movements
——— Confederate
      Troop Movements

CHAPTER FIVE

Vicksburg, 1863

Gʀᴀɴᴛ ᴡᴀs ᴅᴇᴛᴇʀᴍɪɴᴇᴅ ᴛᴏ ʀᴇᴍᴀɪɴ ᴇɴᴄᴀᴍᴘᴇᴅ ᴏᴜᴛsɪᴅᴇ Vicksburg until the town was his. To fall back again as he had after Holly Springs would hurt the nation's already low morale. To divide his army into two widely-separated columns, as he had when he sent Sherman via the river and remained himself in central Mississippi, would require him to give one of the columns to McClernand, the amateur general and professional politician. The only alternative was to keep the army under his direct command on the Mississippi until Vicksburg fell.

Taking the fortified town posed a thorny problem. A direct assault from the river up the Vicksburg bluffs would have to be carried out literally under the muzzles of the Confederate heavy batteries and was dismissed as suicidal. An approach from the north led across the disastrous bottomland of Chickasaw Bayou.

What remained was somehow to get the army onto the interior plateau of Mississippi and thence to approach Vicksburg from the east or south. Yet, reaching that plateau seemed almost impossible.

Vicksburg was the northernmost point where the Mississippi touched the plateau that formed Vicksburg's towering bluffs. South of Vicksburg, the plateau continued to be within easy reach from the river, but that stretch of river was barred by the batteries at Vicksburg. North of the town, a belt of terrain known as the Delta intervened between the Mississippi and the plateau. Low, flat, and laced with bayous, the Delta was a vast expanse of swamp, relieved at intervals by rich cotton plantations perched on sinuous low-lying islands. Tapering to a point near Memphis on the north and again at Chickasaw Bayou on the south, the Delta bulged as wide as sixty miles between those points.

For much of its length, the Delta's eastern boundary was the Yazoo River, which lapped the base of the plateau north of Vicksburg as the Mississippi did south of the town. Ascent of the Yazoo was forbidden by batteries at Haynes's Bluff. Crossing either the Yazoo or the Mississippi would require steamboats. The challenge for the Federals was to get their boats into the Yazoo north of Vicksburg or into the Mississippi south of it, without steaming past either Vicksburg or Haynes's Bluff.

During the first four months of 1863, Grant and Porter tried a series of plans. Grant assigned Sherman to carry out the first such gambit, digging a canal across De Soto Point, the bend of the river opposite Vicksburg, in hopes that the river would divert its course to the new channel and leave Vicksburg inland—its batteries irrelevant. Without much hope of success, Sherman made his plans to carry out Grant's orders. Lincoln had heard of the canal project and was eager to have it pushed as energetically as possible.[1]

Sherman's men dug for six weeks in the hard clay, but even when the Mississippi, raised by spring freshets, broke through the levee and flooded the point, the canal proved insufficient. The same floodwaters overflowed many of Sherman's camps, which his men had to move to the levees, the only remaining dry ground in the vicinity. Sherman assigned other regiments to take up residence in steamboats, while he maintained his own quarters in a house surrounded by water and accessible only via a plank walkway built on top of posts, which connected it to the levee.[2]

Grant's other two corps, McClernand's (formerly Morgan's) Thirteenth and James B. McPherson's Seventeenth, remained encamped farther up the river, engaged in other schemes for getting around the Confederate defenses and reaching the Yazoo above Haynes's Bluff or the Mississippi below Vicksburg. Then on March 16, Grant ordered Sherman to take several regiments on steamboats and support Porter's gunboats in yet another effort to circumvent the Rebel fortifications, this one aimed at the upper Yazoo. The plan, which Porter had suggested, was to enter Steele's Bayou a few miles above Vicksburg. Aided by the high water level in the Mississippi's network of backswamps, the boats could, in theory, proceed up Steele's Bayou to Black Bayou, up Black Bayou to Deer Creek, along Deer Creek to Rolling Fork, down Rolling Fork to the Big Sunflower River, and down the Big Sunflower into the Yazoo. Beyond Steele's Bayou, many stretches of this route were choked with overhanging and fallen trees, which Sherman's infantry would clear.[3]

Sherman caught up with Porter on Deer Creek, and the admiral explained that he planned to press ahead rapidly but wanted Sherman's troops to clear Black Bayou of obstructions, as it was the worst stretch he had covered so far. The squat, heavy ironclads had shouldered their way through, sometimes pushing aside fallen trees as large as twelve inches in diameter, but the transports would never be able to duplicate that feat. For these more fragile riverboats, the infantry would have to clear the way. Sherman distributed his troops at various points along Black Bayou, and they got to work.[4]

Throughout March 19, Sherman heard the booming of Porter's heavy guns sounding more frequently than should have been necessary to drive off Confederate guerrillas. Late that night, an African-American reached Sherman's headquarters carrying a note Porter had written on tissue paper and hidden in a roll of tobacco. The admiral was in trouble. Deer Creek was so narrow and twisting that his gunboats could not maintain steerageway, and sailors had to stand on the open decks and fend off the bank with poles. The flotilla had come to a place where the Rebels had felled trees across the creek and were present in sufficient numbers to prevent sailors from venturing on deck. Unable to go forward or back, the fleet was in danger of being captured, and Porter contemplated blowing up his vessels and striking out through the swamps with his crews in hopes of reaching Union lines. In this extremity, he had dispatched the courageous contraband with the hidden message for Sherman.

Sherman immediately dispatched Colonel Giles Smith with all the troops available at Hill's Plantation, some eight hundred men, to cut their way through to Porter and to assure him that Sherman would be coming with the largest force he could gather. Then, left almost alone at the plantation, Sherman paddled a canoe down Deer Creek to Black Bayou. Four miles from Hill's Plantation, he encountered the steamboat *Silver Wave* carrying more troops for the work details. Sherman went aboard and directed the transport on a wild run up Black's Bayou, crashing against trees until the boat's upper works were a shambles. They stopped to pick up the scattered work details in an empty coal barge towed behind the steamboat. A mile and a half from Hill's the *Silver Wave* could go no farther. Disembarking, Sherman led his men on a candlelight march through the canebrakes.[5]

After resting briefly at Hill's, they set out again at daylight, Sherman leading them on foot. The troops double-quicked most of the way, with occasional rests, sometimes wading waist-deep through swamps and covering twenty-one miles by noon. They drove off a Confederate detail attempting to fell trees across Deer Creek behind the gunboats, then swept forward in line of battle and cleared the Rebels out of the woods and cotton fields from which they had been harassing the gunboats. An officer of Smith's command gave Sherman a locally acquired horse, and the general mounted bareback and galloped ahead of his men along the creek-side road to join a much-relieved Porter. As he passed the gunboats, the sailors poured out onto the decks to cheer him.[6]

With cover from Sherman's infantry, the gunboats withdrew safely. In the course of the episode that came to be known as the Steele's Bayou expedition, Sherman had taken far more personal risks than was customary for a general of his rank—traveling alone in a canoe at night in the enemy's country and personally leading a column marching to encounter the enemy—but the expedition displayed the energy and loyalty to comrades that were the traits that had already made Sherman Grant's favorite subordinate. Those qualities, in whatever manner they might be displayed, were applicable to any war, before or since.

The Steele's Bayou route for circumventing Vicksburg was clearly a failure, and the same outcome had emerged for each of the other routes proposed for reaching either the upper Yazoo or the Mississippi below Vicksburg without confronting the Rebels' heavy guns. Sherman had always been frank with Grant in his preference for a resumption of an overland approach like the one Grant had tried from northern Mississippi the preceding fall and abandoned after Holly Springs. He contended that the army now had the strength to make that plan work, and the approaching summer, with its lower water levels in all the regions' streams, would be the ideal time to do it.

Having shared these thoughts informally with Grant and his staff on a number of occasions, on April 8, Sherman committed them to paper in a letter to Grant's chief of staff, Colonel John A. Rawlins. His purpose in doing so was two-fold: not only to press his views on the army commander but also to encourage Grant to demand a similar statement from each of his other two corps commanders, particularly John McClernand. Everyone knew that the political general was still working overtime to undermine Grant in Washington. Sherman feared that when the coming campaign was over, whatever plan Grant might pursue, McClernand would announce that he had had a better one that would have brought greater and easier success. Getting him on record in support of any particular plan would forestall that. Grant, however, thought it unnecessary and took no action. Whatever Grant might decide, Sherman assured him in his letter that he would give "the same zealous cooperation and energetic support" as he would if the plan were his own.[7]

Grant was already making vigorous preparations for a scheme of his own. If Vicksburg's batteries could not be dodged, then they must be braved. Obtaining Porter's agreement to run the fleet past the Vicksburg batteries, he made plans for the transports to follow several nights later. The necessary vessels would then be where Grant wanted them: in the Mississippi River below Vicksburg. The army would work its way south through the swamps on the west bank, and the boats would ferry the troops across to within a short hike of the undefended bluffs that edged the long-sought interior plateau.

The first running of the batteries was scheduled for the night of April 16. It was a risky undertaking. Grant and Porter were proposing, in effect, to call the Rebel gunners' bluff, to see if the destructive power of the Confederate guns matched the deterrent value that had, with a couple of exceptions, prevented vessels from attempting such a feat throughout the winter. Anticipating losses, Sherman had his men drag four yawls across De Soto Point, and when the time came for the dash past the batteries, all four were waiting in mid-channel below Vicksburg, with Sherman in one of them, ready to fish ship-wrecked sailors out of the water. Only one boat sank, the transport *Henry Clay.* Six nights later Sherman had his lifeboats back out in the river for the second running of the batteries and picked up crewmen from the sunken steamer *Tigress.*[8]

Grant was now free to take the next step in his plan. On April 20, he issued his first formal orders to the army for the downriver movement. McClernand's Thirteenth Corps, whose camps were closest to the road that wound through the west-bank swamps, was to march first, followed by McPherson's Seventeenth. Sherman would bring up the rear with the Fifteenth, and it would be some time before the muddy, difficult road was clear of the preceding units so that his men could take up the march. Grant sent a note suggesting that Sherman feint against Haynes's Bluff to draw Confederate troops north of Vicksburg and away from Grant's landing point south of the town.

Grant explained that he was reluctant to order the move. Well aware of Sherman's bad relations with the press, Grant knew that if Sherman feigned an attack and then withdrew, the newspapers would likely publicize it as another repulse for Sherman. Explaining his concern, Grant left the decision up to Sherman. His friend's reply was a virtual snort of contempt at all ink-stained busybodies. If Grant thought the feint helpful, Sherman would carry it out, newspapermen be hanged. He took a force up the Yazoo on steamboats and put on a show of preparing to attack the Rebel batteries. Subsequent intelligence revealed that Pemberton had responded by countermarching troops previously dispatched to Vicksburg's southern approaches.[9]

By May 1, the roads leading south were clear, and Sherman's command took up the march down the west bank. During the march down the west bank, they passed a number of fine plantations, most of which had seen rough use by the troops that had already passed. Sherman particularly noticed the plantation of a Mr. Bowie—brother-in-law to proslavery but pro-Union Maryland politician Reverdy Johnson—whose acquaintance Sherman had made in Washington more than a decade before when Johnson was a member of Zachary Taylor's cabinet along with Thomas Ewing. The Bowies had absquatulated and were nowhere to be found. That was always a mistake if one wished to preserve one's property from a passing Civil War army, and when Sherman arrived a soldier was sitting in a fine silk chair on the front porch, resting his feet on the keys of a piano, while the slaves made off with more of the furniture through the back door. Sherman put a stop to both activities. He assigned some of the slaves to straighten up the house and one of them to inform any passing soldiers that the owner was a relative of Reverdy

Johnson and the place should be spared. Then, he went on his way. Before nightfall, the Bowie house had burned to the ground. Sherman was not sure whether it was his soldiers or the slaves who had torched it. As was often the case, Sherman wished to spare Rebel property but did not wish it badly enough to inconvenience his operations by detaching troops to guard it.[10]

The next day, May 7, Sherman moved his corps across to the east bank of the Mississippi, still following in the wake of Grant's other two corps. Grant had planned to swing east before moving north against Vicksburg, so as to get clear of the difficult, ravine-slashed terrain near the edge of the plateau and approach Vicksburg directly from the east. As he did so, however, Pemberton directed the garrison at Jackson, then a single large brigade under Brigadier General John Gregg, to harass the fringes of Grant's march. On May 12, Gregg mistakenly plowed into the head of McPherson's Seventeenth Corps column near Raymond, Mississippi and got a severe drubbing for his trouble, but the incident convinced Grant that Jackson needed to be neutralized. It was a transportation hub, supply depot, and obviously, a potential base for any Confederate efforts to assemble a relieving army for Vicksburg. He assigned McClernand's Thirteenth Corps to watch Pemberton's main army while Sherman's and McPherson's corps veered farther east to deal with Mississippi's capital.

On May 14, the two corps attacked Jackson with overwhelming force. General Joseph E. Johnston, Pemberton's superior and commander of all Confederate forces between the Appalachians and the Mississippi, had by then arrived in Jackson, but the Rebel forces present were minimal and could do no more than fight a brief delaying action before abandoning the town. In this relatively easy victory, Sherman's troops bagged two hundred prisoners and ten field guns.[11]

About 4:00 P.M. Grant summoned Sherman and McPherson to meet with him at a large hotel opposite the statehouse. He explained that from intercepted dispatches he knew that Johnston and Pemberton would try to unite their forces. He decided to prevent this with

McPherson's and McClernand's corps. Grant assigned Sherman and his corps the task of rendering Jackson more or less harmless. Slated for destruction were all railroad facilities, the arsenal, a foundry, and various other factories and depots.[12]

After the meeting, Grant and Sherman went together to visit a nearby factory. The staff, mostly young women, had gone right on with their work despite the battle and the arrival of the Union army. They were making tent cloth with the letters *C.S.A.* woven into each bolt of fabric. After watching for several minutes, Grant dryly observed that he thought the women had done enough work. He announced that they could go home now and could take as much cloth with them as they could carry. After they were gone, Sherman's troops torched both the factory and its stockpile of cotton bales waiting to be made into tents for the Confederate army.[13]

The next morning, McPherson's corps marched out of Jackson heading west, to meet Pemberton, while Sherman's troops stayed behind to continue destroying Confederate military, industrial, and transportation assets. Twenty-four hours later, Grant, who was riding with McPherson, received further intelligence indicating that he was getting very close to Pemberton's army. Though he would have liked to have left Sherman to work on Jackson for another day, he decided he had better bring as much of his force together as possible for the impending battle and so sent a dispatch to Sherman to start one of his divisions immediately and follow with the rest of his force as soon as the work in Jackson could be completed. Much to Grant's satisfaction, Sherman had Steele's division on the road within an hour of receiving the dispatch and followed with the rest of his corps later that day. As Grant would later observe, Sherman had done his work in Jackson "most effectually."[14]

As Sherman was leaving town, a very fat man approached him and asked if the Yankees were going to burn his hotel, pointing to a large wood-frame building near the railroad depot. He was, he said, "a good Union man." Sherman dryly observed that he could see that. On the hotel's sign was its name, *Confederate Hotel*, but underneath the word *Confederate* one could still see, faintly painted over, the word *United States*. Sherman allowed that he had no intention of burning the place. Nevertheless, just as the column was marching out of town, the hotel caught fire and burned to the ground. Sherman made inquiries but could never find out just who did it.[15]

It was near sunset that evening when Sherman and his column neared Bolton Station and met one of Grant's staff officers, who gave him the news that Grant had defeated Pemberton that day at the Battle of Champion's Hill; the officer told Sherman that Grant wanted him to push on toward Vicksburg on the Upper Jackson Road, to the north of the rest of Grant's army, and cross the Big Black River at Bridgeport. Sherman pressed forward with his troops the next day, his three divisions marching separately and converging on Bridgeport. They found the bridge destroyed and the far bank defended.

The commander of the lead division, Frank Blair, had a plan to mount a few of his troops on artillery horses and swim them across the river to drive the Rebels off. Sherman, when he arrived, thought this sounded like a bad idea. Once again, as he had on the Steele's Bayou expedition, disregarding his own safety, Sherman crept down to a corncrib near the riverbank, from which he was able to observe the modest Confederate fortification on the other side. He ordered up an artillery battery and had directed several shells into the position when the entire opposing force, a Rebel lieutenant and ten men, stood up and surrendered. Shortly thereafter, Blair's engineers were at work assembling a pontoon bridge across the river by the light of pine bonfires on the banks. Later that evening, Grant stopped by, and he and Sherman sat together on a log and watched Sherman's columns tramping across the swaying bridge. Grant brought Sherman up to date on the progress of McPherson's and McClernand's corps, of which the latter had had a brief but successful fight with the Confederates at Big Black Bridge, south of Bridgeport. There too, engineers were constructing bridges, and the troops were preparing to cross.[16]

By ten o'clock the next morning, May 18, Sherman's corps, advancing on the right of Grant's army, had reached a point from which it could take the Haynes's Bluff defenses from the rear, and Sherman dispatched a regiment of cavalry to scout the place. As he expected, the Rebels had already abandoned it, and the Union troopers made contact with a navy gunboat in the Yazoo River, to whose commander they turned over the formerly Confederate fortifications on the bluff before riding back to report to Sherman. That afternoon, the Fifteenth Corps reached the fortified lines around Vicksburg itself, and its skirmishers began exchanging fire with the Rebels. On orders from Grant, Sherman's corps continued to comprise the army's right, and during the rest of the day and into the night, as his long column came up, Sherman extended his lines farther to the right until they reached the Mississippi River above the town.[17]

Hoping to capitalize on the momentum his army had gained by defeating the Rebels at Champion's Hill on May 16 and at Big Black Bridge on the following day, Grant ordered an attack for May 19. The Confederates still had plenty of fight left in them, however, and most of Grant's army, having filed into its positions during the night before, had had no opportunity to take up the best positions from which to launch their assault or to reconnoiter the extremely rough and often confusing ground over which they were to advance. The attack, when it occurred, was poorly coordinated and had little chance of success. Some of Sherman's troops reached the enemy parapet but could go no farther. Casualties were high.[18]

Grant met with his corps commanders the following day to discuss the situation. They agreed that their men had not really had a fair shot at the Vicksburg entrenchments. The natural strength of the position, situated as it was on steep hills fronting on deep ravines that wound this way and that, had prevented the army from striking with its full weight anywhere except in the vicinity of where the three main roads entered the Confederate lines, and there the defenses were strongest. Grant directed them to make thorough preparations for another assault, to begin precisely at 10:00 A.M., May 22. Over the next two days, Sherman worked hard to get his corps ready. All his artillery was brought up and entrenched to bear on the Rebel lines. Sherman personally reconnoitered his front and selected two points on the Confederate defenses that looked a bit weaker than the others. He would direct his main strength at those, while making "a strong demonstration" along the rest of his lines.[19]

That morning, in preparation for the attack, Sherman took up a position about two hundred yards from the Confederate defenses, concealed in defilade so that by stepping a few feet forward up the slope, he could peer over the crest with relative impunity and see his troops make their attack. The assaulting troops went forward as scheduled, but the result was no better than it had been three days before. Some of Sherman's men reached the outer slope of the Confederate parapet and hung on there for hours, tossing back the grenades the Confederates threw at them and beating off every Confederate attempt to drive them away. Several were later awarded the Medal of Honor for their exploits. Yet, they could not get over the parapet and into the Confederate fortifications, and eventually they had to fall back to positions with better cover.[20]

Not long thereafter, Grant joined Sherman at his observation post. Sherman showed him where his troops had attacked and admitted that they had been repulsed. Grant said things had been much the same on McPherson's and McClernand's fronts. A few minutes later, a courier brought Grant a dispatch from McClernand. His troops had, the note claimed, taken a Confederate strongpoint on the lines and were trying to fight their way forward, but the Rebels were massing their forces against him. Unlike the other two corps commanders, he had not retained a reserve to exploit a breakthrough, and now he wanted Grant to send him reinforcements from the rest of the army and to order Sherman and McPherson to renew their assaults so that the Rebels could not concentrate on his breakthrough.[21]

"I don't believe a word of it," Sherman recalled Grant remarking after showing the note to Sherman. A staff officer standing nearby thought Grant's words were, "If only I could believe it." Sherman responded that the "note was official, and must be credited." "A corps commander would not write a misstatement over his own signature at such a time," the staff officer remembered Sherman saying. "I don't know," Grant replied. Of course, he and Sherman both knew that McClernand, like most politicians, could conceivably write a false statement at any time, but Sherman was alerting Grant to the political ramifications of the present situation. If Grant did not give McClernand the support he requested, then McClernand, who everyone knew had for months been waging a campaign to undermine Grant with his political superiors, would claim that Grant's folly had lost a potential victory. Seeing Sherman's point, Grant reluctantly gave orders for one of McPherson's divisions to reinforce McClernand and for McPherson and Sherman to renew their assaults.[22]

The results were predictable. In fact, McClernand's troops had made no real breakthrough. His assaulting elements had been pinned down on the scarp of the Rebel fortifications. At one point, where the Union preparatory bombardment had battered a small breach in the parapet, a few of McClernand's men made a brief foray into a Confederate redoubt and took a few prisoners. When the reinforcements arrived from McPherson, McClernand employed them with little skill and less prospect of success. An excellent brigade commander was killed, as were a number of his men, and nothing was accomplished. Eventually, McClernand had to admit it and recall the troops.[23]

To renew the assault in his own sector, Sherman repeated the tactics that had failed a few hours earlier, since no others seemed to offer any better hope of success. Once again, troops advancing in linear formation would apply pressure on a broad front, while a fast-moving column aimed at what Sherman thought the most promising point in his sector—a Confederate defensive work known as the Stockade Redan, which could be approached via road and thus allowed the attacking column, in theory at least, to spend a minimum of time exposed to defensive fire.

As his new assaulting column, Sherman selected Brigadier General Joseph Mower's "Eagle Brigade." Mower was one of the most aggressive officers in the army; his brigade took its name from the mascot of one of its regiments, a bald eagle named Abe, who rode into battle perched on a special pole carried by the color guard. "General Mower," Sherman asked, "Can you take those works?" Mower surveyed the Stockade Redan and shook his head slowly. "I can try," he said. "Then do it," Sherman ordered. Mower and his men did try. As with the previous storming party, some made it to the scarp of the Confederate fortifications, and a color bearer of the 11th Missouri planted his flag there. Yet, they could go no farther, and men were falling fast. "This is murder," Sherman said to Mower's division commander, "order those troops back." He did, but some of the men were pinned down and had to wait until nightfall to withdraw. Casualties were significant, but somehow Mower himself came through unscathed. Abe suffered a slight wound.[24]

That night, Grant's headquarters became the informal gathering place for much of the Army of the Tennessee's top brass—most of the corps and division commanders and their staffs, probably including Sherman. Together with Grant's staff, they exchanged bitter reflections over McClernand's performance, which as Grant's chief-of-staff John A. Rawlins put it, had done nothing but add another thousand men to the casualty lists.[25]

The two assaults having failed, nothing remained for Grant and his army but to lay siege to Vicksburg, digging zigzag trenches closer and closer to the Confederate defenses until they could place cannon close enough to breach the parapets—or tunnel under them and blow them up, or overwhelm them with a sudden rush by masses of infantry—or a combination of all three. It was tedious, laborious, and often dangerous work, most of it carried out at night, but the soldiers proved diligent and eager to learn the finer points of military engineering involved. Sherman skillfully oversaw the progress of the works in his sector and pushed them forward aggressively. By the end of the first week of the siege he was ready, in some parts of the line, to plant batteries within eighty yards of the Confederate parapet. When necessary, Sherman was willing to take an axe in his own hands and demonstrate to the volunteer soldiers the finer points of making such pieces of siege work as fascines and gabions. These bundles or cages, made of saplings and sometimes filled with earth fulfilled somewhat the same purpose that sandbags would do in more modern entrenchments.[26]

Colonel John Sanborn had been a lawyer in St. Paul, Minnesota, before the war. At Vicksburg, he belonged to McPherson's corps. One day during the siege, he received an order to assign a hundred-man detail to make fifty gabions and fifty fascines. Unfortunately, neither Sanborn nor any of his subordinates knew what those items were. He had the detail drawn up and was about to order it off into the woods under its puzzled commanding officer when Sherman passed by on his way to check on another part of the front.

Pausing to talk with Sanborn, Sherman must have noticed both officers' perplexity, for he asked the detail commander what task his troops were to perform. The officer handed his written orders to Sherman. "Do you know how to make gabions and fascines?" the general asked. "Do you know what they are?" Sanborn chimed in that he and his men had been in the army less than a year and this was their first siege. Thus, as he euphemistically put it, he and his officers did not "feel very well posted in regard to these matters."

Recognizing the problem, Sherman dismounted and asked for an axe. Thus equipped, he led the detail into the woods and thickets and demonstrated for them the technique of making gabions and fascines by actually making an example of each. Sanborn was especially impressed at Sherman's "not even ordering an enlisted man to do it for him, but doing the work with his own hands." By doing so, he had not only left them well instructed in those two points of siege craft, but as Sanborn put it, "got a hold upon the enlisted men that made them all ready to die for him."[27]

On the evening of June 16, one of Sherman's division commanders, Frank Blair, stormed into his headquarters in a towering rage, waving a copy of the June 13 edition of the *Memphis Evening Bulletin*. The paper included a copy of a lengthy announcement by McClernand to the men of his Thirteenth Corps. Though couched as a congratulatory order to the men, the piece was transparently a work of self-congratulation. Rehearsing at length the events of the campaign, McClernand wrote as if his corps had accomplished them virtually unaided, and he went on to imply strongly that his corps would have triumphed in the May 22 assault if Sherman and McPherson had not let him down. Sherman might stand for this, Blair raged, but he would not, and if Sherman did not take the matter up with Grant, Blair would engage his own considerable political connections, including his brother the postmaster general, and his father, a senior statesman and veteran of the Andrew Jackson administration.[28]

The following morning Sherman wrote a letter to Grant denouncing McClernand's order as "an effusion of vain-glory and hypocrisy." He pointed out that it was not really meant for the troops at all but rather for voters in the North, and he reminded Grant that it was in fact a blatant violation of army regulations, which specified that reports were not to be published without explicit permission. Sherman's letter was the first clue Grant had received of the existence of such a report by McClernand, who had simply neglected to submit it to him. That same day, Grant heard from his other corps commander, McPherson, regarding the same self-congratulatory announcement of McClernand's: McPherson had read the order in another newspaper, a June 10 edition of the *Missouri Democrat*.[29]

When Grant queried McClernand as to the authenticity of the newspapers' copies, McClernand replied that they were indeed genuine and that he stood behind every word of them. That Grant had not received a copy through more accustomed channels had been the result of an oversight by a member of McClernand's staff. Grant was unimpressed. He had finally had enough of McClernand, a marginally competent corps commander, who flirted as constantly with northern voters as he did with insubordination to his commanding officer. Late that same evening—actually 2:00 A.M. the next morning—Grant issued an order relieving McClernand of his command and banishing him from the Army of the Tennessee. As soon as Grant had issued the order, but without his knowledge, wickedly gleeful staff officers had McClernand roused from his sleep to receive it. He departed the next day, raging of the political revenge he would take, but he had exhausted his capital with Lincoln and could accomplish nothing more.[30]

Several days later, Grant received a report that a relieving army under Joseph E. Johnston had crossed to the west bank of the Big Black somewhere above Bridgeport and was threatening to move to the southwest on to the rear of the Union forces besieging Vicksburg. Grant had been expecting Johnston to make some such move and had planned to counter it by entrusting Sherman with a command to face Johnston and prevent his approach to Vicksburg. For that purpose, Sherman would have one division from each of the Thirteenth, Fifteenth, and Seventeenth corps, then besieging Vicksburg, a division of the Sixteenth Corps, brought down from occupation duty in West Tennessee, and the two divisions of the Ninth Corps, dispatched by Washington to make sure that nothing prevented the capture of Vicksburg and its garrison, would join them as well—six divisions in all.[31]

The report of Johnston's imminent approach turned out to be false. The Confederate general was a commander of formidable reputation, and Grant told Sherman that Johnston was the only enemy general whom he feared. Yet, the Rebel general kept his army in central Mississippi, north of Jackson, doing nothing, while the siege of Vicksburg ground on week after week. Sherman had his men construct defensive works near the Big Black River, facing the direction from which Johnston would likely approach, and there he waited confidently for the Rebel to make his attempt. Johnston never did.

During this lull of nearly two weeks, Sherman actively inspected his front but also had time to look up some old acquaintances living in the area. In a small log house near Markham, Mississippi, lived the Klein family. Mrs. Klein was Sherman's brother-in-law's sister's daughter. While in the neighborhood, Sherman occasionally took meals with the family, thereby according their house substantial immunity from pilfering Union soldiers, who thought of Mrs. Klein as "the general's cousin." One day while riding his lines, Sherman learned that the mother of one of his former Louisiana Military Seminary cadets was staying in a nearby home as a refugee from New Orleans and, perhaps rather naively, decided to pay his respects. Finding the house where the lady, Mrs. Wilkinson, was staying, Sherman found her sitting on the front porch with nearly a dozen other women. Introducing himself, Sherman inquired about her son. The young man, she informed him, was inside Vicksburg, a Confederate soldier. And what of her husband, Sherman continued. At this the woman burst into tears. "You killed him at Bull Run, where he was fighting for his country!" Sherman protested that he had not killed anybody at Bull Run, but the whole company of women broke out in wails of lamentation, and Sherman decided to beat a retreat. Some days later, on July 3, however, Mrs. Wilkinson sought Sherman out at his headquarters. She said she knew Vicksburg must soon fall, and when it did, she wanted to visit her son, who would then be a prisoner of war. Would Sherman write a letter for her to Grant, asking that she be allowed to visit the young man? He did, and it had the desired result.[32]

As it had become increasingly apparent that Vicksburg could not hold out much longer, Grant had notified Sherman to be ready to go over to the offensive against Johnston. Grant planned to assault Vicksburg on July 6, and if he carried the place, he alerted Sherman to have on hand sufficient supplies by that time for an immediate advance toward Jackson, in hopes of catching Johnston or driving him out of the state. As it turned out, Vicksburg surrendered on July 4, but Sherman was already prepared, and reinforced by the remainder of the Thirteenth and Fifteenth corps, freed up by the fall of Vicksburg, he marched at once toward Jackson.[33]

The weather was brutally hot. Water was scarce, and the retreating Rebels had killed animals and thrown them into the few ponds and wells so as to render the water unusable. The troops suffered severely, but by July 10, they had reached Jackson and found Johnston at bay there behind entrenchments that the Rebels had strengthened since Sherman had left the city the preceding May. For a week, Sherman's army carried on a sort of mini-siege, pressing closer and closer to the Confederate earthworks while steadily bombarding the town. On the morning of July 17, they discovered that Johnston had evacuated across the Pearl River the night before, and Mississippi's capital fell to the Yankees for the second time. The weather conditions made massive heat casualties likely if the army attempted any hard marching now, so Sherman decided not to pursue Johnston into the piney woods of eastern Mississippi. He notified Grant, who ordered the troops back to the Vicksburg area. By July 27, the several corps had dispersed to separate camps around Vicksburg, Sherman's Fifteenth to the Big Black, near where he had encamped during the latter stages of the Vicksburg siege, and there they continued at rest for the remainder of the summer.[34]

Vicksburg was one of the most important Union victories of the war. It severed the Confederacy from its trans-Mississippi states with their abundance of supplies, reopened the Mississippi River to the commerce of the Midwest, and provided a major morale boost for the Union. The campaign also cemented the relationship of Grant and Sherman. Sherman had disagreed with Grant but supported him enthusiastically, showing the kind of loyalty Grant valued above all other qualities. He had proven to be the most dependable of Grant's subordinates and the one Grant chose for positions of the greatest responsibility. The two men's trust in each other was complete. As Grant continued to rise, Sherman would rise with him. The qualities that made Sherman Grant's most trusted lieutenant—loyalty, trust, and the ability to work effectively with a superior—are timeless factors that transcend the particular circumstances of the Civil War and distinguish successful command partnerships in any conflict.

CHAPTER SIX

From Memphis to Meridian, 1863–1864

THE VICTORY AT VICKSBURG BROUGHT PROMOTIONS FOR THE top generals who had been involved in it. For Sherman, that meant a step up to brigadier general of the regular army to go along with the commission he already held as major general of volunteers. The award made no difference in Sherman's authority within the present overwhelmingly volunteer army, but it was a promise of a good career in the regulars when the war was over.[1]

The thoughts of many in the late summer of 1863 were beginning to turn hopefully to the end of the war. Vicksburg had been the great victory, but Union arms had prospered elsewhere as well. Rosecrans had, simultaneously with the closing days of the Vicksburg siege, led the Army of the Cumberland in maneuvering Bragg's Confederate army almost completely out of Tennessee, and

Union armies had checked Rebel counteroffensives at Helena, Arkansas, and Gettysburg, Pennsylvania, on the very day Vicksburg surrendered. Peace seemed much closer than it had only a few weeks before.

With this in mind, Henry Halleck, from his post as general-in-chief in Washington, wrote to Sherman on August 29 asking for his private thoughts on the state of southern society, so that Halleck might be able to use them in advising Lincoln on the political reconstruction of the rebellious states. As has been the case in wars since, and is likely to be in others yet to come, an American general was being asked for his advice on how the government should deal with a hostile conquered populace. In a letter dated September 17, Sherman made his reply. "The valley of the Mississippi is America," he premised his argument, and therefore the states of Mississippi, Louisiana, and Arkansas were key to Reconstruction.

From his familiarity with the culture and society of the region, Sherman sketched several different classes of inhabitants. The poor and middling whites, Sherman believed, were a political cipher. They liked to think that democratic institutions gave them the real power in society, but in fact those institutions were simply the means by which the wealthy planters manipulated them. The planters were generally hostile to the Union, and they could not be reasoned with. They might, however, be made to see their self-interest in the reestablishment of legitimate government, provided Union forces won a couple of additional major victories in the region. The most dangerous class was composed of the "young bloods," as Sherman called them—aggressive, vigorous, young men skilled at arms, fond of war, and bored with the prospect of peace. Union forces would either have to "kill these men or employ them," Sherman maintained, apparently suggesting their enrollment in the post-war army. In any case, he believed it was no use trying to set up civil government in any of these places before the rebellion was thoroughly crushed.

Above all, Sherman emphasized, the North must make a clear demonstration that the nation had the necessary will to enforce its legitimate authority. "I would banish all minor questions," he wrote, "assert the broad doctrine that as a nation the United States has the right, and also the physical power, to penetrate to every part of our national domain, and that we will do it—that we will do it in our own time and in our own way; that it makes no difference whether it be in one year, or two, or ten, or twenty; that we will remove and destroy every obstacle, if need be, take every life, every acre of land, every particle of property, every thing that to us seems proper; that we will not cease till the end is attained." Those in the North who hindered the war effort should be deprived of the rights of citizenship, and as for the Rebels, "I would not coax them, or even meet them halfway, but make them so sick of war that generations would pass away before they would again appeal to it."[2]

Much in Sherman's letter was prescient, both about what it would take to win the war and what it would take to establish a lasting peace, but it flew in the face of Lincoln's long-cherished desire to offer generous peace terms and to set up reconstructed state governments as soon as possible, even before the guns had fallen silent. It was curious, therefore, that Halleck telegraphed Sherman that he had let Lincoln read the letter and that the president had asked him to get Sherman's permission to publish it. The last thing Sherman wanted was to have his views bandied about in the newspapers, and so he declined. What Lincoln may have been thinking is hard to say, unless perhaps the president was, in effect, hoping to play a sort of "good cop, bad cop" routine on the South.[3]

Sherman availed himself of the mid-summer lull in operations to bring his family down to visit him in the camps of the Fifteenth Corps near the Big Black River, east of Vicksburg. Ellen, Minnie, Lizzie, Willie, and Tom arrived and spent several weeks. Willie, who was nine, was a special favorite of his father and also of his father's headquarters guard, the Thirteenth U.S. Infantry. The soldiers adopted the lad as a sort of mascot and made him an honorary sergeant, and Willie, who took more interest in his father's profession than any of his siblings, reveled in watching the battalion drill.[4]

The idyllic interlude ended abruptly when on September 22 a dispatch arrived with news from another front. Rosecrans and his Army of the Cumberland were in trouble. After several weeks of idleness that summer, Rosecrans had advanced skillfully and maneuvered Braxton Bragg's Rebel army out of Tennessee. Bragg received reinforcements from other parts of the Confederacy, however, and as Rosecrans pursued him into Georgia, the Rebel general had turned at bay and dealt the Army of the Cumberland a defeat in the September 18–20 Battle of Chickamauga. His confidence shattered, Rosecrans pulled his army back into Chattanooga, Tennessee and allowed Bragg to occupy key high ground around the town, all but cutting it off from supplies.

The first dispatch Sherman received called for him to send a division back to Vicksburg for shipment up the river to Memphis and the overland journey to reinforce Rosecrans in Chattanooga. The following day, Grant summoned Sherman to Vicksburg in person and informed him that he would be sending him to Chattanooga with his entire Fifteenth Corps. By September 25, Sherman was back at his camps on the Big Black, giving the necessary orders to prepare for the march. Within two days, the last of his divisions had set out for Vicksburg, and on the twenty-eighth, it embarked and started up the river.[5]

By that time, Sherman too had embarked, along with his family, taking passage in the steamboat *Atlantic* bound for Memphis. The family was standing by the rail, watching Sherman's old camps at Young's Point glide by, when Sherman noticed that Willie did not look well. Sherman queried his son, and the lad admitted that he felt sick. His mother bundled him off to bed, and an army surgeon on board was summoned to examine him. The verdict was typhoid fever. As the boat labored upstream toward Memphis, the illness grew worse until the surgeon had to inform Sherman that his son's life was in danger and that they needed to get to Memphis as soon as possible for additional medical help. They arrived October 2, carried Willie to the Gayoso Hotel, and summoned the city's most experienced physician. All proved for naught, however, as Willie died on the evening of October 3, with his family gathered around him.[6]

Sherman was profoundly grief-stricken and reproached himself for having brought his family into a sickly region in the midst of summer. In fact, it was probably the proximity of the military camps Willie loved that had caused the boy's death. Sanitation was still poorly understood, and sickness dogged the armies, taking more soldiers than the enemy's bullets. Sherman had little time to mourn. He purchased a metallic casket, and on October 4, the Thirteenth U.S. Infantry conducted a military funeral, escorted the casket to the dock, and placed it aboard the steamer *Grey Eagle* for the trip back to Ohio, accompanied by Ellen and the three other children who had been on the visit to their father.

Sherman remained to carry out his duties, but that night, unable to sleep, he sat up to pen a note of thanks to the commanding officer of the Thirteenth. "The child that bore my name," he wrote, "and in whose future I reposed with more confidence than I did in my own plan of life, now floats a corpse, seeking a grave in a distant land, with a weeping mother, brother, and sisters, clustered about him." For himself, Sherman said he sought no sympathy. "On, on I must go, to meet a soldier's fate, or live to see our country rise superior to all factions." He asked that the battalion receive his thanks for the honor they had shown Willie and promised that each of them would always have a special place in the hearts of the Sherman family.[7]

The same day that he arrived in Memphis and took Willie to the Gayoso, Sherman received dispatches that told him of the rapidly developing military situation. His lead division had already departed Memphis by train for Corinth, ninety-six miles closer to Chattanooga and as far as the railroad was running. Another division was even then boarding trains in Memphis for the trip east, while a third was debarking from steamboats at the docks, and the last was on its way up the river from Vicksburg. For several days, Sherman continued to expedite his troops' passage through Memphis. Finding a shortage of locomotives and rolling stock on the railroad between Memphis and Corinth, he decided it would be faster for one of his divisions to make the trek on foot and gave orders for John M. Corse's division to march along the road that paralleled the rails.

Two days later, October 11, Sherman himself set out in a special train along with his staff, headquarters personnel, and the Thirteenth U.S. Infantry. Eight miles out, the train caught up with the columns of Corse's division and rolled past the toiling foot-sloggers. Around noon, they rattled past the little station of Colliersville, twenty-six miles out of Memphis. About a half mile beyond the station, however, a dozing Sherman was jerked awake by the train slowing and stopping. Exiting his car, he encountered the commander of the Sixty-sixth Indiana, which comprised the Colliersville garrison, informing him that his pickets had just been driven in and that it appeared a large force of Rebel cavalry was about to attack the station. Sherman ordered the train to back up to the station and went about deploying his scant forces for a defense; holding the brick depot building, a small earthwork about two hundred yards away, the railroad cut near the station, and some nearby trenches. One of his staff officers found a supply of extra rifles at the depot and distributed them to the clerks and orderlies to assist in the defense. Minutes before the Rebels cut the telegraph wires, they got a message back up the tracks toward Memphis, exhorting Corse to come on quickly.

The fight started only a few minutes later and lasted for three or four hours. Confederate artillery damaged the locomotive, and the Rebels at one point succeeded in getting into the train, capturing several horses, including a favorite of Sherman's, and attempting to set the cars on fire before Federals drove them out. At last the Confederates broke off their attack as Corse's division doubled-quicked into view. After a day's delay to repair the battered locomotive, Sherman was back on his way.[8]

Arriving in Corinth, Sherman set about carrying out the mission that Halleck had assigned him by way of Grant. Because Rosecrans's supply lines were already badly strained, Halleck believed an additional supply conduit would be needed, and Sherman was to provide it by repairing the Memphis and Charleston Railroad—much damaged by Confederate guerrillas—as he worked his way east. It was a slow process, and there was no telling when, if ever, Sherman would have reached Chattanooga at this rate. In general, the Rebel guerrillas could break the line as fast as Sherman's men could mend it.

As it was, Sherman had been at work supervising repairs on the railroad for about a fortnight, when on October 27, he received messages that changed his mission. Grant had been promoted to command of the newly-created Military Division of the Mississippi, comprising the departments of the Tennessee, the Cumberland, and the Ohio, and had been specially charged with the task of rescuing Rosecrans in Chattanooga and then Major General Ambrose Burnside's Army of the Ohio, which seemed to be similarly besieged at Knoxville. Sherman had anticipated this, writing Grant before leaving Memphis that such a promotion was probably in the offing and that he should not hesitate to accept it. No sooner was Grant promoted than he saw to it that his friend Sherman received a corresponding promotion to command of the Army of the Tennessee. Grant by then was in Chattanooga, and he sent Sherman a brief dispatch by courier: "Drop all work on Memphis and Charleston Railroad, cross the Tennessee, and hurry eastward with all possible dispatch toward Bridgeport, till you meet further orders from me."[9]

Sherman started his troops at once. His lead division was at Florence, Alabama, and it pressed on up the north bank of the Tennessee River followed by the other three. High water and a burned bridge on the Elk River required a detour upstream into Tennessee to find a good crossing point. Then, from Decherd, Tennessee, Sherman's men set out on the hard pull up and over the Cumberland Plateau, then down the other side to arrive November 13 at Bridgeport, Alabama, thirty-five miles west of Chattanooga, having come more than 170 miles from Florence. The weather had often been rainy and the roads deep with mud, while on the Cumberland escarpment the men sometimes had to pick up their wagons and lift them over rock ledges in the badly eroded roadbed.[10]

Waiting for him in Bridgeport, Sherman found a dispatch from Grant directing him to proceed to Chattanooga in person for a conference. Sherman took passage on one of the small steamboats then shuttling supplies into Chattanooga and rode as far as Kelly's Ferry. There he disembarked and found orderlies waiting for him with one of Grant's own horses. Thus mounted, he rode into Chattanooga on the evening of November 14. On Sherman's arrival, the normally undemonstrative Grant welcomed him warmly, smiling broadly and offering him a cigar. Then he motioned Sherman to the most comfortable chair in the room, a rocker. "Take the seat of honor, Sherman." The subordinate demurred that such a place naturally belonged to Grant. Not to be put off, Grant responded, "I don't forget, Sherman, to give proper respect to age." "Well, then," said Sherman, who was twenty-six months older than Grant, "if you put it on that ground, I must accept."[11]

The next morning, Sherman and Grant went out to survey the situation from the Chattanooga fortifications. Surrounding the town at a distance somewhat more than a half mile from the Union fortifications were hills—half of them, in an arc from southwest to northeast, held by Bragg's Confederates. On towering fourteen-hundred-foot Lookout Mountain and all along the length of six-hundred-foot-high Missionary Ridge, the tents, batteries, and trenches of the enemy were in plain view—stretching from near the river below the town almost to the river above it. "Why, General Grant," Sherman blurted, "You are besieged." "It is too true," Grant replied modestly, though in fact he had already scored a major success by opening a good supply line into Chattanooga. He also had a plan for lifting the siege and dealing with Bragg's annoying Confederates.[12]

Not surprisingly, Sherman and his men figured prominently in that plan. Grant was frustrated with the Army of the Cumberland and its new commander, Major General George H. Thomas, who had recently replaced Rosecrans. Many of the army's horses had starved during the recent siege, and the rest were too weak to pull guns, caissons, and supply wagons. This made the Army of the Cumberland almost completely immobile. Thomas was the antithesis of the can-do attitude Grant had instilled in his own Army of the Tennessee and which Sherman and his troops personified. The Army of the Cumberland had never functioned that way, and Thomas was not about to change his cautious, methodical ways and his low tolerance for risk. Grant also suspected that the Army of the Cumberland's morale might be low after the defeat at Chickamauga. Everything it seemed to lack, Sherman's corps possessed in spades. Grant wanted Sherman to open his offensive with a nighttime crossing of the Tennessee River above Chattanooga and then a rapid movement to gain the north end of Missionary Ridge beyond the Confederate flank. Then, Sherman would come crashing down on that flank right along the length of the ridge.

Together with Grant and other officers, Sherman rode through the hills behind Chattanooga to a vantage point near the river from which he could see the north end of Missionary Ridge across the Tennessee Valley. He studied the terrain and the planned crossing point as carefully as he could, given that Confederate pickets were posted on the far bank. Eager to get back to his troops and put the plan in motion, Sherman hurried back to Kelly's Ferry in hopes of catching the boat that evening. He was too late. Rather than wait another twenty-four hours, he got the local commanding officer to give him a rowboat and four soldiers to man the oars. With these, he traveled through the night, occasionally taking a turn at an oar to spell one of his men. At Shell Mound, he picked up a new crew, and continuing on, he reached Bridgeport by morning.[13]

He immediately put his command in motion, but the next few days were ones of intense frustration for Sherman. The roads were muddy; the pontoon bridge at Brown's Ferry was shaky; and Sherman got his supply wagons entangled in his column. Despite his and his soldiers' strenuous efforts and their pride in their ability to march quickly, it was November 23 before they reached their as-signed jumping-off point. For Grant, nagged by repeated telegrams from Washington demanding action, it was a difficult wait.

That night, Sherman's troops carried out a well planned and ex-ecuted landing on the left bank of the Tennessee, seizing the Confed-erate pickets before they could raise the alarm. The operation proceeded smoothly and rapidly from one phase to the next, as Sher-man's men secured the beachhead, laid a pontoon bridge, and swarmed across the river en masse. The Confederates, distracted by a diversionary attack against Lookout Mountain at the other end of their line, made no reaction. By midday November 24, Sherman had three of his divisions in line and moved out to take the north end of Missionary Ridge. Heavy clouds dimmed an already short late-No-vember afternoon, but before the light faded, Sherman's lead ele-ments had reached the high ground he had identified from the opposite bank as the northern terminus of Missionary Ridge.[14]

Here, they ran into the first hitch of the operation. Missionary Ridge was not the simple landform it appeared from a distance. It was in reality a lumpy range of hills, linked to each other by inter-vening saddles. The hill Sherman's troops took first was separated from the rest of the ridge by a saddle so low as to make it a freestand-ing eminence known locally as Billy Goat Hill. Here, Sherman's men encountered the first Confederate reaction: skirmishers of Major General Patrick R. Cleburne's division, whom Bragg had dispatched to the north end of the ridge when he learned of Sherman's advance. The Federals easily drove Cleburne's skirmishers over Billy Goat Hill, down the other side, across the low saddle, and up the slope of the next hill, the first hump of the ridge proper. Then, as night was falling, they dug in and waited for morning. Cleburne's men dug in on the ridge's next significant hump, an eminence known as Tunnel Hill, since the tracks of the Western and Atlantic Railroad passed through a tunnel below it.[15]

That evening, Sherman informed Grant by dispatch that his men were astride Missionary Ridge and had almost reached the tunnel. Back from Grant came orders to renew the advance at dawn. Grant's other forces would strike at the Confederate center and left, but his main reliance was on Sherman rolling up the Rebels' right flank.[16]

Sherman advanced as ordered early on the morning of November 25 but soon ran into trouble. His men had no difficulty getting on the ridge, but they had moved along it scarcely two hundred yards when they ran up against Cleburne's position on Tunnel Hill, where the curious nature of the terrain became apparent. On the rolling farmlands where Civil War armies fought most of their battles, a ridge-top position was strong to its front and weak on its flanks, but in this mountainous terrain, the reverse was true. A line atop steep-sided Missionary Ridge would have been easier to attack by massed frontal assault than by the sort of crest-line advance Sherman was now attempting. The ridge top sloped up gradually toward Cleburne's position, giving the Confederates a perfect field of fire. It was narrow enough that scarcely two hundred men could advance abreast along it, facing an equal number of entrenched defenders— members of what was recognized as the best brigade in Bragg's army. Additional attackers, attempting to wrap around Cleburne's hilltop position, would be at a severe disadvantage on lower ground where they could not see their fellow attackers or coordinate their assaults. Cleburne, on the other hand, could see and quickly respond to every Union movement. Additional Confederates on a spur to the rear of the ridge laid down a crossfire that ruled out any wider flanking movement.

Hour after hour, Sherman's troops battered at the impregnable position, at times coming close enough to engage the defenders in hand-to-hand combat across the breastworks. At other times, they delivered such a heavy and accurate fire that few Rebels dared show themselves above their breastworks. Yet, the attackers could not overcome the inherent advantages of the Confederate position. The compact defensive perimeter—with good all-round visibility— allowed Cleburne, the most talented of the Confederacy's division commanders, to display all of his adroitness in parrying Sherman's efforts to extend the fight around to the front side of the ridge. Skillfully timed counterattacks gave Cleburne the initiative and allowed him to mass his forces against the separate components of Sherman's advance, separated as they were by the curve of the ridge's lower slopes.

Watching the fight from a hilltop vantage point between Chattanooga and the ridge, Grant by mid-afternoon realized that progress was impossible on Sherman's front and ordered Thomas to advance his Army of the Cumberland and take the line of rifle pits at the base of the front side of the ridge as a first step toward taking the main Confederate line on the crest. A very reluctant Thomas arrayed twenty-three thousand men along the plain in front of the ridge and ordered them forward without clear direction as to where they were to halt. They took the lightly-manned rifle pits, and then, coming under fire from the ridge top, their officers ordered them up the slope. The steep hillsides that had looked so forbidding were in fact creased with numerous ravines that spoiled the Rebels' field of fire. Compounding the Confederates' distress, their comrades fleeing the rifle pits were only a few yards ahead of the pursuing Federals, further impeding defensive fire. The Confederate lines broke in several places and soon collapsed into a complete rout.

The Battle of Chattanooga was a splendid victory for Grant but a profound frustration for Sherman. Assigned the star role in Grant's grand offensive, he had been unable to get into position as quickly as he and Grant had hoped. Then, after a promising beginning, his attack had stalled against an impregnable position—while Thomas, more or less in spite of himself, scored the major breakthrough that carried the day.

The only bright spot in all of this was that it reinforced the strength of the relationship Sherman and Grant had established. Sherman made no attempt to shift blame for his disappointing performance, and Grant generously took the blame for Sherman's slow march (he felt he should have instructed his friend not to take his wagons)—and sincerely, if inaccurately, credited Sherman's persistent attacks with drawing additional Confederate troops to his end of the ridge, and thus facilitating Thomas's success. The level of mutual trust between Grant and Sherman provided the foundation for them to become the most effective command partnership of the war and offered an example of cooperation that would apply not only to generals in future wars but to almost any human endeavor.[17]

The victory at Chattanooga did not quite close the campaign. At Knoxville, about one-hundred miles away, Major General Ambrose Burnside reported his smaller Army of the Ohio to be similarly besieged by a Confederate force under Lieutenant General James Longstreet. Lincoln, deeply pained at his inability, through much of the war, to aid the staunchly Union-loyal population of East Tennessee, was intensely concerned lest the Rebels reconquer this region that Federal troops had liberated only three months before. His constant telegraphic reminders left Grant in no doubt that the commander-in-chief expected immediate action for Burnside's relief. Grant would have preferred to give Sherman and his weary men a break after their long march from Mississippi, but he could trust no other commander to get there promptly and deal with Longstreet. Sherman undertook the task without complaining and made the difficult march through the deepening winter.

Longstreet decamped on his approach without waiting to give battle to Sherman, who promptly made contact with Burnside. He found the Army of the Ohio commander with his officers in the midst of a turkey dinner. In fact, the situation in Knoxville had never been dire but had only been made to seem so by Burnside's inadequacy as a commander. With East Tennessee secure, Sherman took his command back to Chattanooga, but despite the two hundred-mile winter tramp on what turned out to be a fool's errand, no distrust or animosity developed between Sherman and Grant.[18]

With the campaign in East Tennessee finally ended, Grant moved his headquarters to Nashville, and shortly thereafter Sherman came to confer. He wanted Grant's permission to carry out a large-scale raid from Vicksburg deep into the interior of Mississippi to destroy the Confederate base and transportation center at the town of Meridian, about twenty miles from the Alabama line. Along the way, he planned to destroy many of the resources that might otherwise support Confederate raids against Union holdings along the Mississippi. This would allow the transfer of the entire Army of the Tennessee to Georgia for the opening of the main spring campaign of 1864. Grant readily agreed to Sherman's proposition.[19]

That evening, the two generals, along with several other officers, decided to take in a performance of *Hamlet*. Sherman was quite a fan of Shakespeare and therefore was all the more disappointed when the quality of the performance turned out to be abysmal. The soldiers who made up most of the audience were catcalling loudly, and Sherman was muttering harsh criticisms under his breath, when Grant quietly suggested that the party of officers should leave before the soldiers recognized them and felt encouraged to riot. Back out on the street, Sherman suggested they find a restaurant that served oysters. They found one and had just received their food when the proprietor announced that they would have to leave the premises at once, as the restaurant was closing in conformity with military curfew. Ruefully but quietly they left, closing an evening they would remember wryly for many years.[20]

After a furlough in Lancaster to spend Christmas with his family, Sherman returned to Mississippi early in January 1864, ready to carry out his planned raid against Meridian. His old Fifteenth Corps was still in its camps in northern Alabama after participation in the Chattanooga and Knoxville campaigns, but he drew two divisions from the Sixteenth Corps, which had been performing occupation duty in West Tennessee, and two more from the Seventeenth, which had, since the fall of Vicksburg, been serving in a similar capacity in western Mississippi. Hurlbut would command the two divisions of the Sixteenth Corps and McPherson those of the Seventeenth, with Sherman in overall command. By February 1, all of the assigned forces had rendezvoused at Vicksburg and were ready for the start of an operation that was to become a pattern for some of Sherman's greatest campaigns during the coming year.

During the preceding weeks, Sherman had taken care to obtain good intelligence about the Rebel defenses in Mississippi and knew that Confederate general Leonidas Polk had two divisions of infantry and two of cavalry, one of which was deployed toward Memphis and would probably be occupied by a force of Union cavalry—under Brigadier General William Sooy Smith—advancing from that city in cooperation with Sherman's march. Sherman also knew the location of each of Polk's other divisions and had information indicating that Polk was not expecting an attack. Maintaining a degree of secrecy that was surprisingly uncommon in the Civil War, Sherman kept his own troops in ignorance of their destination even after the march began, and he saw to it that the word was put out to the civilians along the way that the ultimate objective was Mobile.[21]

On February 3, Sherman's two corps marched east from Vicksburg, McPherson's Seventeenth Corps on the right and Hurlbut's Sixteenth on the left. The march was unopposed until they reached the Big Black River, about ten miles out, on the afternoon of the first day. Thereafter, Confederate cavalry hovered around them like bees after a honey-robbing bear—and with about as much effect. Mostly they were a nuisance, inflicting only a handful of casualties and hardly impeding the march at all. Both Union columns camped that evening about four or five miles beyond the Big Black.[22]

Despite the presence of the Rebel horsemen, Sherman's men were able to gather foodstuffs extensively from the countryside through which they passed. This was an essential part of Sherman's program—both to enable him to move his army rapidly, unimpeded by extensive wagon trains or the need to protect a supply line, and also to deplete the surplus food supplies of the region, and thus, make future Confederate operations there more difficult. Neither the hovering Rebel cavalry nor Mississippi civilians who tried to conceal their food stocks could foil Sherman's foragers, and the troops lived high on hams and other cured meat as well as fresh hogs, cattle, and poultry.

This was just as Sherman wanted it. When a local woman asked him to post a guard over her smoke house to keep soldiers out of it during the passage of the army, Sherman responded in what was by now his classic style: since Southerners "had brought the war on themselves, they must bear the consequences." The men in the ranks heartily approved of the sentiment and the policy. "Bully for Sherman," an Illinois soldier wrote in his diary the night after overhearing the general's exchange with the woman.[23]

Averaging just less than ten miles per day despite the need to forage and the nuisance of the Confederate cavalry, the expedition reached Jackson on February 6, and for the third time, Sherman captured Mississippi's capital. His stay was more brief this time, only a single day, but his men plied torches more freely, as a number of buildings went up in flames. Still, many structures survived unscathed, including the statehouse. The nickname "Chimneyville," which both soldiers and civilians began to apply to the town, was always an exaggeration.[24]

Next morning, they left Jackson and crossed to the east bank of the Pearl River, into country Union armies had not hitherto penetrated. Yet, they maintained their pace. Public buildings, warehouses, depots, factories, and railroad facilities blazed along their route, as did smaller numbers of gin houses and barns and an occasional private dwelling. As was to become the pattern in such marches, however, the soldiers scrupulously refrained from violence against civilians.

By the evening of February 12, the expedition had come more than seventy miles from Jackson, reaching the crossroads hamlet of Decatur. Due to the limitations of eastern Mississippi's scant network of roads, both corps were marching on the same thoroughfare by this time. Hurlbut's rearguard passed through the village late in the day, with McPherson's vanguard still four miles behind. Sherman personally detached one of Hurlbut's regiments and posted it at the crossroads, there to remain until McPherson's column came in sight. Then, he went into a nearby house, had some supper, and went to bed. He was awakened by the sound of gunfire outside. The commander of the regiment he had left at the crossroads had seen several members of McPherson's staff riding up the road and had considered himself relieved. After his departure, a lightly-guarded wagon train of Hurlbut's command happened by and drew an attack by Confederate cavalry. In the midst of the pandemonium, Sherman sent a staff officer hurrying up the road to recall the regiment and was preparing to hole up in a corncrib for a desperate defense along with the rest of his staff, when the timely return of the missing troops put an end to the cavalry foray.[25]

The expedition marched into Meridian on the afternoon of February 14, still having encountered no resistance from Rebel infantry. Sherman gave his men the following day to rest and then put them to work wrecking the town's capacity to support Confederate military operations. Each corps had a sector assigned to it, and the work went methodically. Once again, factories, an arsenal, and numerous warehouses went up in flames—along with more than one-hundred miles of railroad ties on tracks stretching in four directions from the town, the corresponding rails being heated over the roaring bonfires and bent around trees. The wrecking crews put paid to nearly two dozen locomotives along with about that many bridges, culverts, and trestles. When the work was done, Sherman could write in his report, "Meridian, with its depots, store-houses, arsenal, hospitals, offices, hotels, and cantonments no longer exists."[26]

The return march to Vicksburg differed little from the outward leg of the journey. No infantry disputed their passage, but cavalry harassed them more or less continuously. The men lived off the land and generally fared well, save when they passed over districts whose food supplies they had depleted on the outbound journey a few days before.

To its rear, the column grew a long and ever-increasing tail of African-American refugees fleeing slavery. As the army passed through an area thick with plantations, many members of the large slave community decided to abandon their homes and follow the blue-clad soldiers to freedom. The road was difficult for them, and at its end were the camps of the Freedmen's Bureau, a federal agency that strove valiantly but not always very effectively to improve the lot of the former slaves. In the abstract, Sherman was hostile to these contrabands, as they were called, and his writings include a number of appalling racist statements. Yet, his actual behavior toward African-Americans and his treatment of them when he encountered them personally was at least as benevolent as that of the average Union general. As was often the case with Sherman, he tended to talk more gruffly than he acted.

The expedition reached Vicksburg on March 3, having completed a march of more than two hundred seventy miles and having destroyed an immense amount of Confederate war-making infrastructure. The Meridian Campaign had been a striking success. It fully accomplished its goal of hamstringing any future Confederate offensive operations against Union outposts and shipping along the Mississippi, and it also demoralized the Mississippi populace while demonstrating the ease with which a Union army could sustain itself in the southern interior. Sherman would not forget the lessons he had learned in the operation and before the year was out would be applying them on a much larger scale. The campaign pointed the way to a style of warfare that would aim not at the enemy's armies but rather at his supplies, transportation, factories, and other means of supporting those armies in the field. It was not an idea totally new within the history of warfare, but during the course of 1864, Sherman would learn to apply it to the circumstances of modern war.

William Tecumseh Sherman

John Sherman

Ulysses S. Grant

Thomas Ewing, Jr.

James B. McPherson

George H. Thomas

Confederate fortifications outside Atlanta

John A. Logan

Sherman on the siege lines outside Atlanta

*The Atlanta
Car Shed*

*The ruins of the
Atlanta Car Shed*

Ossabaw Sound from Fort McAllister

Edwin M. Stanton

CHAPTER SEVEN

From Chattanooga to the Chattahoochee, 1864

By the spring of 1864, Sherman stood poised to launch his first major campaign as an independent field commander. He had learned much in the preceding years as a subordinate and in smaller, briefer independent commands. At Chickasaw Bayou, a year and a half earlier, he had learned that even the Union armies, with the might and manpower of the North behind them, were not sufficient to win the war purely by means of attrition. Before the attack there, he had quipped that the Union was bound to lose five thousand men before taking Vicksburg and the loss might as well occur at Chickasaw Bayou. In the attack, he had lost fewer than two thousand but had ended no closer to Vicksburg than he had begun. At that rate, no advantage in numbers or materiel would ever suffice to put down the rebellion.

Ironically, it was Grant, the mythical master of attrition, who taught Sherman the warfare of maneuver. The Vicksburg Campaign of May 1863 was the war's finest exemplar of maneuver warfare, a virtual clinic in the operational art. Again and again Grant had moved not against Pemberton's strengths but against his weaknesses, and he had consistently gathered information, interpreted that information to gauge the operational situation, decided what needed to be done, and implemented his decisions well before Pemberton could get through the same steps. The Confederate commander had looked helpless while Grant, who had fewer total troops in Mississippi, fought and won a succession of five battles, in each of which he had more troops present on the field than did the outmatched Confederate general. Sherman had been skeptical of Grant's plan, but by the time it was over he had freely confessed its brilliance. In his own great campaign, which would be played out on a stage more than twice the size of the Vicksburg Campaign, Sherman would make good use of the lessons Grant had taught him, but he would apply maneuver warfare in ways adapted to the conditions in Georgia and to his own personality.

The Meridian Campaign, though smaller in extent and in numbers than the one about to begin, taught Sherman lessons about logistics. The fact that his army had been able to live off the southern countryside reassured him about the precarious rail line from the front back to Louisville that was his only other source of supply. In a letter to Grant written a few weeks before the launch of the spring campaign of 1864, Sherman wrote, "Georgia has a million of Inhabitants. If they can live we should not starve." If the enemy should cut his supply line, he would have no difficulty—and no compunction—about having his troops take what they needed from the countryside.[1] Nevertheless, he made elaborate plans for protecting his long rail line, providing for a series of small garrisons in blockhouses and prepositioned repair parties with plenty of spare rails, ties, and trestle components, and he gave strict orders reserving the railroad for the shipment of military supplies only.[2]

On March 18, Sherman arrived in Nashville to assume command of the Military Division of the Mississippi from Grant, who was about to leave for Washington to assume his own new duties as general-in-chief of the Union armies. The two generals conferred at length in Nashville, and then Sherman accompanied Grant on his journey as far as Cincinnati for further discussions. By the time they parted, Sherman had a clear understanding of what Grant expected of him in the coming campaign. Two major Confederate armies remained in the field: Robert E. Lee's Army of Northern Virginia, defending Richmond, and Joseph E. Johnston's Army of Tennessee, defending Atlanta. Grant saw those two armies as the Confederacy's center of gravity and key to survival. If they could be destroyed, the war would be won. He therefore planned to direct George G. Meade's Army of the Potomac in going after Lee's army, while Sherman directed the three smaller armies in the Military Division of the Mississippi in attacking Johnston.[3]

Grant was concerned that the Union armies in the two separate theaters of the war would operate "like a balky team, no two ever pulling together." Hitherto the Union's war effort had been characterized by such episodes as Rosecrans sitting idle while Bragg had reinforced the Confederates in Mississippi against Grant, and Meade operating blandly in Virginia while Lee had detached troops to Bragg for Rosecrans's discomfiture at Chickamauga. Now it was to be different. Each Union army must keep constant pressure on its opposing Confederate army to prevent the detachment of reinforcements for other fronts. Grant and Sherman's close friendship and high competence insured that the two main Union forces, directly under their supervision, would pull steadily together—although, as events were to show, several smaller Union armies, carrying out subsidiary operations, were to come to complete balks despite the best efforts of Grant and Sherman. On their two immediate commands would rest almost the whole weight of defeating the Confederacy.

In his offensive against Johnston, Sherman's supply line and axis of advance would be the Western and Atlantic Railroad, which ran from Chattanooga about one hundred twenty miles southeast to Atlanta. The Confederate general had entrenched his army in a well-nigh impregnable position along Rocky Face Ridge, a north-northeast-to-south-southwest lying landform athwart the Western and Atlantic, about thirty miles southeast of Chattanooga, just north of the town of Dalton, Georgia. The railroad passed through the ridge at a gap known as the Buzzard Roost, for its high and precipitous sides. Johnston, whose instincts as a general were entirely passive, longed for nothing more than to have Sherman attack him in his chosen position.

That was something Sherman had no intention of doing. Rather, he planned to maneuver his three armies so as to avoid Johnston's strength—the position on Rocky Face—and strike at his chief vulnerability: the Confederate's own long railroad supply line, the same Western and Atlantic, running from Dalton all the way down to Atlanta. The fact that Rocky Face Ridge slanted across the Western and Atlantic made a maneuver around Johnston's southern flank especially attractive, and that was just the maneuver Sherman planned to launch. George H. Thomas's Army of the Cumberland, sixty-one-thousand strong, would start the campaign from Chattanooga, advance against Rocky Face directly, and feign a frontal assault. The fourteen-thousand-man Army of the Ohio, commanded by John M. Schofield, would set out from Knoxville, march south and threaten Johnston's northern flank on Rocky Face Ridge. Meanwhile, the Army of the Tennessee would strike the main blow. Now commanded by James B. McPherson, the army that had been Sherman's own would set out from its camps in northern Alabama and march east to seize the town of Rome, Georgia. A valuable industrial target in its own right, Rome would give McPherson a position from which he could pose an intolerable threat to Johnston's communications. The Rebel general would have to retreat, and then all three of Sherman's armies would join and pounce on the fleeing Confederates.[4]

Problems arose before Sherman and his generals could put the plan in motion, and these problems related, in one way or another, to Union efforts to secure the Mississippi Valley in preparation for the main 1864 campaign against Johnston and Atlanta. Sherman's own Meridian Campaign had been the first, and, though it was successful, it left a negative aftereffect for Sherman's spring campaign. Congress had promised soldiers whose enlistments were to expire in 1864 that they could have a thirty-day furlough at home if they reenlisted early for another three years of service. Most soldiers in the high-morale Army of the Tennessee had done so, and the army therefore owed them furloughs. The Meridian Campaign had taken place during the time that most other units were enjoying their reenlistment furloughs, and most of the reenlisting regiments that had composed Sherman's force in the campaign were still entitled to furloughs when they got back. The furloughs, coupled with travel time and other delays, meant that two divisions of the Seventeenth Corps would not be rejoining the Army of the Tennessee until June, more than a month after the start of the campaign.

The other Mississippi Valley campaign had not been under Sherman's command, and it had not been a success. Politician-turned-general Nathaniel P. Banks, commanding the Department of the Gulf, led an expedition up the Red River with a mixture of goals—including securing the Mississippi Valley, seizing cotton for the hungry mills of New England, showing the U.S. flag somewhere in the general vicinity of Texas (beyond which French emperor Louis Napoleon was staging an adventure in Mexico) and, perhaps most of all, boosting Banks's own future chances for the presidency. Culminating in fiasco at the Battle of Mansfield, Louisiana on April 8, 1864, the expedition accomplished none of its goals. The two divisions of the Army of the Tennessee on loan to Banks for the campaign performed well and saved his army from a still worse drubbing, but Banks managed to detain them so long that they were too late to join Sherman's campaign against Atlanta. To compound the trouble, Grant and Sherman had expected Banks to carry out a campaign against Mobile simultaneous with Sherman's against Atlanta. Instead, the politician-general's Red River farce so delayed him that the campaign against Mobile did not take place that year.[5]

In response to these problems, Sherman felt the need to modify his campaign plan. Instead of the thirty-thousand to thirty-five thousand men he had anticipated, the Army of the Tennessee, minus four of its divisions, would now number about twenty-four thousand men. In making its deep turning movement aimed at Rome, it would be exposed to possible reaction by the Confederate forces of the Department of Mississippi and Alabama—the same forces Sherman had faced but never met during the Meridian Campaign. Instead of being occupied in the defense of Mobile, these Confederates, under the command of Lieutenant General Leonidas Polk, would be free to fall on McPherson's flank. If at the same time Johnston turned on him, the plight of the much-weakened Army of the Tennessee would be desperate. Sherman therefore opted to alter his design. He would keep the Army of the Tennessee closer to the potential support of his other two armies. Rather than sending it directly from northern Alabama to Rome, Sherman would route it instead through north Georgia, fairly close to Chattanooga—and thus, execute a closer, less daring turning maneuver by marching around Johnston's left via a pass in Rocky Face Ridge called Snake Creek Gap.

Thomas had discovered Snake Creek Gap the previous winter while carrying out a feint against Johnston, and he had suggested that Sherman send him with his Army of the Cumberland to turn Johnston through the gap. Sherman recognized the impracticality of the suggestion. The Army of the Cumberland was far too large to move quickly and stealthily enough to evade Johnston's notice, even if Thomas had been the commander to direct such a move. Moreover, Thomas's forces had been directly in Johnston's front, and their sudden disappearance would have been sure to excite notice. Using the Army of the Tennessee made much more sense, both because of its more supple size and its proven record of maneuver warfare in Mississippi and because of its starting position in northern Alabama.

Sherman set May 1 for the opening of the offensive, and the armies began to move right on time. By May 4, the Army of the Tennessee reached the Chattanooga area, and on the eighth, it entered Snake Creek Gap and camped that night in the three-mile-long valley. Johnston remained oblivious to the threat developing beyond his left flank. The following day, McPherson's troops resumed their advance, hindered only by a weak screen of Confederate cavalry, which they drove before them with ease. Emerging from the eastern side of the gap, they continued another three miles to within a mile of the town of Resaca, located where the tracks of the Western and Atlantic crossed the Oostenaula River. There, the Confederates had only a single brigade to dispute the advance. Sherman's orders were for McPherson to break the railroad and then pull back into a strong defensive position near the mouth of Snake Creek Gap. With his supply line cut, Johnston would have to retreat. When he did, McPherson could tear at his flank, while Sherman would be on his heels with the other two armies to complete his destruction.[6]

At this point, the plan went awry. McPherson's leading elements were within a few hundred yards of the railroad when he gave the order to halt and pull back. Lacking cavalry for scouting, McPherson worried that Johnston, whose army was less than twenty miles away by good roads, would turn and fall on the isolated Army of the Tennessee. Accustomed to the more aggressive leadership of Grant and Sherman, McPherson's troops were puzzled, but by the next morning, May 10, he had them entrenched in the mouth of Snake Creek Gap, awaiting an attack from Johnston that never came. Disappointed that McPherson had failed to cut the railroad, Sherman decided to move most of the rest of his force through Snake Creek Gap, leaving a single corps in front of Buzzard Roost to distract Johnston's attention. By the evening of May 11, however, Leonidas Polk had arrived at Resaca with the Confederate troops of the Department of Alabama and Mississippi, henceforth to function as a third corps of Johnston's army. Polk's presence greatly reduced the chances of seizing Resaca and trapping Johnston north of the Oostenaula, and Johnston had soon pulled his forces back to join Polk around the town.[7]

Sherman's first turning maneuver of the campaign had been a partial success. He had failed to catch and destroy Johnston's army, as he had hoped, in an operation that would have won the entire campaign in a matter of days and gone far toward ending the war. Yet, he had forced Johnston to abandon the impregnable position along Rocky Face Ridge and to fall back some twenty miles closer to Atlanta. That the maneuver had not produced the results Sherman had hoped for was largely attributable to McPherson, who was in his first major operation as an army commander. When Sherman arrived at Snake Creek Gap late on May 12, he greeted the Army of the Tennessee's commander warmly, but remarked, "Well, Mac, you have missed the opportunity of a lifetime."[8]

By that time, the front had stabilized with Johnston holding defensive lines stretching in an arc from the banks of the Oostenaula west of Resaca around to a position northeast of the town. During the next several days, the opposing armies probed at each other, precipitating some serious fighting as the commanders tried each other's flanks and searched for weak points in the opposing line. Sherman had no intention of settling into the sort of war of attrition in which his opponent, on the entrenched defensive, would have all of the advantages. He decided on another turning movement. Once again the armies of the Cumberland and the Ohio would hold Johnston's attention while the Army of the Tennessee went around his flank—this time by means of a cross-river assault in pontoon boats against light Confederate forces holding the south bank of the Oostenaula west of Resaca. The operation was successful, and with Sherman's troops once again threatening to cut his line of communication, this time south of the Oostenaula, Johnston abandoned Resaca and retreated across the river during the predawn hours of May 16.[9]

Sherman immediately put his forces in pursuit, as Johnston continued his retreat for more than forty miles. The opposing armies skirmished frequently and had a minor clash at Adairsville. A few miles farther on, at Cassville, Johnston contemplated launching a major counterattack, then thought better of it and continued his retreat. Sherman's troops were advancing more rapidly than Johnston could formulate and implement his offensive plans. Constantly foiled and unable to regain the initiative, the Confederate general halted his retreat only after placing the Etowah River between himself and Sherman's pursuing armies. Sherman pulled up on the north side of that stream to give his armies a few days to rest and to repair the more than seventy miles of Western and Atlantic track they had taken over so far that month. In less than three weeks, Sherman, in a dazzling display of maneuver warfare, had advanced two-thirds of the way from Chattanooga to Atlanta with minimal casualties.[10]

The next stage of the advance, however, promised to be much more difficult. The thirty miles between the Etowah and the Chattahoochee rivers comprised the best defensive terrain between Chattanooga and Atlanta. The Blue Ridge Mountains separated the rivers, and in the midst of the range, Johnston had arrayed his army at Allatoona Pass, in a defensive position even stronger than the Buzzard Roost. It offered the Confederate general an opportunity for exactly the type of warfare he most desired to fight: a contest of attrition in which his enemy would attack him head-on over ground that gave Johnston all the advantages—if only Sherman would cooperate.

Sherman knew the terrain he would have to cross. During his assignment in Georgia in the 1840s, aiding in the investigation of the Seminole War claims, he had ridden over this ground, and he now proved to have an exceptional memory for topography. He would make no effort to approach Allatoona Pass frontally, as Johnston hoped, but would instead make another turning maneuver, wider and bolder than the previous two that had taken his armies past Rocky Face Ridge and the Oostenaula. From Cartersville, his troops would leave the Western and Atlantic, with its promise of steady supply, and strike out by country roads due south toward Dallas, Georgia, more than fifteen miles from where the tracks ran through Allatoona Pass. If the plan worked, Johnston would, at least, have to abandon his strong defensive position and fall back, perhaps all the way through the belt of mountains to the Chattahoochee River. Better still, it might allow Sherman to trap Johnston's army or to defeat it in a battle in which Johnston would have to fight without overwhelming advantages of terrain.[11]

To counteract the temporary loss of supplies by rail, Sherman had his armies take with them twenty days' rations either in wagons or on the hoof and directed that strictly supervised foraging parties gather such food as they could from the countryside through which the armies would pass. Compactly arranged armies, moving slowly in the presence of the enemy, could never hope to gather all their food by foraging, especially in this rugged country with few farms, but everything they could pick up would help to eke out the stocks in the wagons.[12]

Sherman had his troops on the march again on the morning of May 23—Army of the Ohio on the left, Army of the Cumberland in the center, and Army of the Tennessee on the right—and each column crossed the Etowah without opposition. Beyond the river, the road led over a range of hills. A dispatch found on a captured Confederate courier revealed that Johnston had learned of the movement and might be expected to respond, so the advancing columns had to be cautious, wary of possible ambush. Sherman's troops encountered the enemy—a force of Confederate cavalry—at the crossing of Pumpkin Vine Creek, a few miles north of Dallas, on the afternoon of May 25. Leading elements of the Army of the Cumberland easily drove the cavalry, but shortly thereafter encountered Confederate infantry in force near a crossroads marked by the presence of a little Methodist meeting house called New Hope Church. The advance ground to a halt amid heavy fighting.[13]

Johnston had succeeded in blocking Sherman's turning maneuver and achieving once again a situation in which his troops could stand on the defensive behind breastworks, which, by this time in the war, both sides hastily prepared whenever they halted. During the week that followed, the armies fought a series of inconclusive actions in the thick woods and rugged terrain around Dallas, fights that were individually known as the Battles of Dallas, Pumpkin Vine Creek, New Hope Church, and Pickett's Mill. Many of the troops referred to the vicinity as "the Hell Hole." Sherman probed for weaknesses in Johnston's line and found none. Johnston made a probe or two with his own troops, with similar results. The side defending breastworks always won. The side advancing across open ground always suffered heavy casualties.

After several days of this, Sherman saw the futility of the endeavor, as well as the growing difficulty of supplying his now stationary armies in this position, and he began trying to edge his way around Johnston's eastern flank for a lunge back toward the Western and Atlantic. Johnston hindered this all he could, but by June 5, Sherman had regained the railroad—not, as he had hoped, at Marietta or below, but rather at Acworth, six miles below Allatoona but thirteen miles above Marietta and twenty-three miles from the crossing of the Chattahoochee. This time, Johnston had made his most successful counter to one of Sherman's turning movements: blocking the advance of the Union armies at Dallas and forcing Sherman to return to the railroad supply line that narrowed the scope of his operations to a corridor Johnston had a better chance of defending. Yet, even against such skillful opposition, Sherman had still achieved the most crucial element of his purpose in making the turning maneuver in the first place. He had pried Johnston out of the strongest defensive position between Chattanooga and Atlanta, and Allatoona Pass was now firmly in his control.[14]

Despite this success, Sherman was still only about halfway through the belt of mountains between the Etowah and the Chattahoochee, and the next obvious problem would be gaining the other half. At first, it seemed that would be easy. Sherman thought perhaps Johnston would continue his withdrawal all the way to the Chattahoochee, but the Confederate was showing more tenacity now than he had earlier in the campaign. This country offered him an abundance of the kind of strong defensive positions he loved. One that particularly appealed to him was on a group of high hills just south of Big Shanty (now Kennesaw), five miles from Acworth—Lost Mountain on the west side of the railroad, Pine Mountain in the center, and finally Brush Mountain east of the tracks.

On June 10, Sherman advanced his armies beyond Big Shanty, pressing up against the Rebel lines. For the next several days, he worked at extending his lines beyond Johnston's, bending them around the Confederate flanks to enfilade key positions, all under the watchful eyes of the Rebels on the heights. On June 14, Sherman trained his field glasses on the crest of Pine Mountain and saw a party of Confederate officers surveying his armies' movements. Their ability to do so piqued his frustration at being thus stymied in his advance toward Atlanta. "How saucy they are!" he exclaimed and gave orders that his artillery should take the mountaintop under fire and at least make the Rebel brass take cover. In fact, Sherman's gunners already had the crest zeroed in, and even before his orders, watchful artillery officers had noted the cluster of gray uniforms and were preparing to open fire.

The Confederate officers on Pine Mountain were Johnston himself along with his two top corps commanders, Leonidas Polk and William J. Hardee. When Sherman's guns opened up, the Rebel generals immediately moved toward cover, but Polk did not move fast enough. The second or third shot scored a direct hit on the Army of the Tennessee's senior corps commander.[15]

It was one of the worst shots fired for the Union cause during the entire course of the war. Polk, though an 1827 West Point graduate, had never served in the prewar army. Resigning upon graduation, he had entered the Episcopal priesthood, rising to the rank of bishop during the thirty-four years that followed, without taking any interest at all in military matters. When the Civil War began, Polk had cadged an appointment as major general, direct from civilian life, from his old West Point crony Jefferson Davis. Polk was one of the two old academy comrades for whom Davis retained a regard verging on veneration throughout his life (the other was Albert Sidney Johnston, who had died at Shiloh). Yet, Polk's incompetence and willful disobedience had consistently hamstrung Confederate operations west of the Appalachians, while his special relationship with the president made the bishop-general untouchable. Had Polk lived, Davis would almost certainly have put him in Johnston's place within a matter of weeks—with results that could only have been spectacularly good for Sherman and perhaps shortened the war by months.

Of course, Sherman could have imagined scarcely any of this when he gave his order for a bombardment, and in any case, Polk was popular with the Confederate rank and file, who were demoralized by his death. When intercepted semaphore signals brought Sherman the news, he took grim satisfaction. "We killed Bishop Polk yesterday," he wrote in a dispatch to Secretary of War Edwin M. Stanton on June 15, "and made good progress today."[16]

The progress of which Sherman wrote included the acquisition of Pine Mountain. His stretching and flanking tactics had paid off at least to that extent, allowing his artillerists to place so much enfilading fire on the mountaintop that Johnston, who that day had had a gruesome personal demonstration of its effectiveness, ordered his troops to evacuate the position. Two days later, the same tactics achieved an even greater success, obliging Johnston to abandon his elevated position and fall back several miles to a position anchored on a ridge called Kennesaw Mountain. Sherman followed and pressed Johnston's lines closely, looking for a weakness or another opportunity to gain leverage on a flank, but a week went by without success.[17]

Sherman grew impatient. He could not seem to outstretch Johnston's defensive lines. In his frustration, he complained, "Johnston must have full fifty miles of connected trenches." That was an exaggeration but seemed a trivial one. Sherman could not get around the Confederate flanks. He was loath to repeat the wide turning maneuver he had used to get around Allatoona Gap, entailing as it did the logistical nightmare involved in releasing his hold on the railroad. He would not take that risk again if he could avoid it. If narrow maneuvers would not dislodge Johnston and wide maneuvers were out of the question, the only other option seemed to be a reversion to the sort of head-on tactics that had served Sherman poorly at Chickasaw Bayou. He surmised that perhaps Johnston had thinned his lines in order to stretch them so far. A frontal assault might break through. Such tactics had worked for Thomas at Missionary Ridge and might work again.[18]

On June 24 Sherman gave his orders for the assault. Elements of the Army of the Tennessee would assault Confederate lines on the lowest of the three summits of Kennesaw Mountain, a peak known as Pigeon Hill, on the right of the mountain's profile as the Union troops faced it. At the same time, the Army of the Cumberland would launch its attack against the entrenched Rebel lines on the rolling ground farther to the right. Simultaneously, the Army of the Ohio would feint against the extreme Confederate left. Sherman gave his commanders two days to get their troops into position and set the date of the assault for June 27.[19]

When the troops advanced, their defeat was quick and unequivocal. They were never close to scoring a significant breakthrough. Even without the advantage of Kennesaw Mountain, the Confederate lines—the same sort of well-built entrenchments both armies were now constructing wherever they halted for a few hours—proved all but impregnable. Losses among Sherman's troops totaled some twenty-six hundred men, including two of the Army of the Cumberland's most popular and talented brigade commanders. It was the worst day of the campaign for Sherman's armies.[20]

Thomas growled that a repetition of the assault would destroy the army, but that was hyperbole. In fact, the losses of Kennesaw Mountain, though the worst Sherman's armies suffered in any one battle between Chattanooga and the Chattahoochee, would scarcely have equaled those of a serious day's fighting for the Army of the Potomac in the campaign Grant was then waging in Virginia. The disastrous assault at Kennesaw stood out largely because it was the only time during this campaign when Sherman departed significantly from his preferred reliance on maneuver to force his opponent out of strong defensive positions. Had he done otherwise—had he waged a relentlessly aggressive campaign of the sort Grant was then waging in Virginia and against a comparably skillful and combative opponent—it is doubtful whether national morale could have stood the additional losses, coming on top of those in Virginia. In this way, Sherman showed a more modern approach than Grant in keeping his casualties down to a level that a democracy could more readily accept in a people's army, though it must be said that in doing this he did not, like Grant, have to deal with Lee.

While McPherson's and Thomas's armies were making their futile attacks against Kennesaw and the nearby Confederate trenches, Schofield, in making his feint against the Confederate left, found a way to turn Johnston's flank and threaten Confederate supply lines below Marietta, well south of Johnston's position. Learning of this, Sherman immediately made plans to cut loose of the railroad below Allatoona and strike out with his whole force toward Fulton, a rail station ten miles below Marietta and scarcely two miles from where the railroad crossed the Chattahoochee River. He gave orders that all of the armies' wagons be well filled with provisions in preparation for the temporary loss of his own supply line. Thomas grumbled that it was too dangerous to abandon their supply line again, but Sherman believed he had no alternative if the advance was to continue. Grant was counting on him to keep pressure on Johnston so that the latter would not be able to send troops to aid Lee in Virginia.

The movement began on July 2, with the Army of the Tennessee pulling out of its position on the Union left and marching behind the Army of the Cumberland and the Army of the Ohio to pass beyond the Union right as the lead element of the turning maneuver. Before the other two armies had time to follow, Johnston, as Sherman had expected, perceived the movement and put his own army in retreat. Watching through a tripod-mounted telescope in front of his headquarters at dawn on the morning of July 3, Sherman saw

Thomas's skirmishers make their way up the slopes of Kennesaw and find the crest undefended.

Sherman knew at once that Johnston's army must be in full retreat and gave urgent orders for his own troops to take up the pursuit. The Confederates would be vulnerable in retreat, and Sherman did not know of any place Johnston could turn and make a stand north of the Chattahoochee, fifteen miles from the crest of Kennesaw. This might well be the chance Sherman had been looking for ever since Snake Creek Gap—an opportunity to force Johnston to give battle on open ground, outside of entrenchments, and in circumstances favorable to Sherman's larger force. When he felt that the lead cavalry division and even some of his leading infantry were not pursuing aggressively enough, Sherman was furious and demanded more energetic action.[21]

To Sherman's surprise, his troops ran up against solidly entrenched Confederates at Smyrna, just six miles below Marietta and halfway between that town and the Chattahoochee. This was unexpected on two counts. First, Johnston had, unbeknownst to Sherman, had his engineers direct vast gangs of slaves in constructing this elaborate defensive position where none would otherwise have existed north of the Chattahoochee. Second, Sherman had not believed that a general as cautious as Johnston had shown himself to be would turn and offer battle, even from strong entrenchments, with his back to a major river.

Indeed, Sherman still did not quite believe it. Thinking that Johnston could not be doing more than making a desperate temporary stand in order to gain time to get his wagons and equipment across the Chattahoochee, Sherman directed Thomas to press Johnston in front while McPherson and Schofield sought ways of crossing the river above and below the Confederate position. When Thomas did not seem aggressive enough, Sherman prodded him with orders to attack fiercely and drive the Rebels back. This time Thomas was right, as Sherman soon discovered when he went forward to make a personal reconnaissance. Climbing to the second story of a house on the Union skirmish line, he surveyed the impressive defensive works in front of him, "one of the strongest pieces of field fortification I ever saw," he would later write. While he made his observations, several shells struck the house, and Confederate marksmen across the way were constantly peppering it with rifle bullets. Sherman somehow remained unscathed.[22]

Content now to let Thomas continue applying firm but cautious pressure to the Confederate lines around Smyrna, Sherman placed his hopes in Schofield's and McPherson's efforts to maneuver around the Confederate flanks and reach the Chattahoochee above or below Johnston's bridgehead fortifications. In fact, both generals were successful, and Sherman's troops soon controlled the Chattahoochee Valley both above and below Smyrna. By this point in the campaign it was easy to predict what would follow. Sherman would maneuver around Johnston, and Johnston would retreat. The only way to prevent that sequence from playing out again as it had all the way from Rocky Face Ridge would have been for Johnston to seize the initiative. That would have entailed giving Sherman battle on open ground, which was exactly what Sherman had been hoping for—and Johnston striving to avoid—ever since the campaign started.[23]

Sherman designated Schofield to make the crossing, and on July 9, Schofield did so, well above Smyrna with little opposition. The rest of Sherman's armies followed. That night, Johnston evacuated the north bank of the Chattahoochee and withdrew almost to the outskirts of Atlanta. From hilltops on the north bank of the river, Sherman's men could catch glimpses of the city, nine miles away.

With the crossing of the Chattahoochee, the Atlanta Campaign entered a new stage. Sherman's armies had successfully crossed all three of the great river barriers—the Oostenaula and the Etowah, as well as the Chattahoochee—that had at the beginning of the campaign stood as obstacles to their advance. All of the mountainous terrain between Chattanooga and Atlanta was now also behind them.

With the Rebel army backed up against Atlanta, the Confederate commander no longer had the space needed to maneuver away from Sherman—unless he gave up Atlanta, something Johnston seemed each day more and more likely to do. As would soon become apparent, Jefferson Davis had very different ideas.

CHAPTER EIGHT

From Peachtree Creek
to Atlanta, 1864

BY MID-JULY, SHERMAN HAD MANEUVERED JOHNSTON BACK ninety miles from Dalton, Georgia, to the northern outskirts of Atlanta—across three major rivers and a mountain range—while suffering only a single significant tactical repulse at Kennesaw Mountain. Only the relatively minor obstacle of Peachtree Creek still stood between Sherman and Atlanta. He had achieved his successes not by brute force but by skillful maneuver, moving not against the enemy's strengths but against his weaknesses, and he intended to continue that system. "Instead of attacking Atlanta direct, or any of its forts," he wrote to Chief-of-Staff Henry W. Halleck in Washington, "I propose to make a circuit, destroying all its railroads"—and thus compelling the Confederates to abandon it.[1]

The fact that Atlanta, and not Johnston's army, was the main target of his operations represented a subtle change from the program that Grant had set down for him and that he had loyally embraced that spring. Whereas Grant not incorrectly saw the Confederacy's major armies as its vital center of gravity, Sherman realized that the rebellion could also be brought to its knees by blows against its transportation and industrial capacity. Instead of destroying armies in the field, Sherman tended to think in terms of destroying the enemy society's ability to field armies. Without ever announcing to Grant or anyone else a formal change of policy, perhaps without quite realizing it himself, Sherman had shifted his focus from the destruction of Johnston's army to the capture of Atlanta as an end in itself.

After his leading elements had crossed the Chattahoochee on July 9, prompting Johnston's withdrawal from his entrenched bridgehead north of the river, Sherman paused to rest his troops, repair the railroad behind him, accumulate a reserve of supplies, and strengthen his bridgeheads on the south bank. Then, on July 17, he began his movement toward Atlanta. As he had promised Halleck, this was no assault on the Rebels' fortified lines. Instead, Sherman planned to cut the railroads that supplied the city and the army defending it. Thus, while Thomas approached Atlanta from due north and Schofield from the northeast, McPherson would take his Army of the Tennessee to the east side of the city and destroy the Georgia Railroad. This would not only break one of the city's supply lines but also help to seal off any rapid reinforcement of Atlanta from Virginia, which Grant had telegraphed to warn Sherman was a possibility.[2]

Advancing from the Chattahoochee, Sherman's troops met only light opposition. The plan proceeded without difficulty, and McPherson's troops reached the Georgia Railroad seven miles east of Decatur on the afternoon of July 18, cut the telegraph, and began tearing up the tracks, moving steadily westward, toward Atlanta. By evening, McPherson's men had wrecked some four or five miles, burning the ties, heating the rails over the fires, and bending them around tree trunks or telegraph poles in what would soon be called "Sherman neckties." Sherman was almost surprised at the easy success of his movement and the lack of Confederate response. "It is hard to realize that Johnston will give up Atlanta without a fight," he wrote in a note to Schofield that day, "but it may be so," he concluded hopefully. "Let us develop the truth."[3]

The next morning, Sherman received interesting news. A Union spy came out of Atlanta bringing a local newspaper with a report that Jefferson Davis had two days earlier relieved Johnston and replaced him with corps commander John B. Hood. Young Hood—thirty-three years of age—was a native Kentuckian and an adopted Texan who had been a West Point classmate of both McPherson and Schofield. Sherman consulted the latter, who informed him that the new commander of the Army of Tennessee was "bold even to rashness, and courageous in the extreme." Sherman and Schofield agreed that Davis's action in replacing an army commander in such circumstances indicated strong dissatisfaction with Johnston's policy of retreat. Hood had to know that he was expected to fight, and Sherman sent word to his three army commanders to be on the alert against possible attack.[4]

The three armies continued their gradual advance toward Atlanta, the Army of the Tennessee all the while continuing to work on the Georgia railroad. By late afternoon, Union lines had closed to within a couple of miles of the city on both the north and the east. Then, at about 4:00 P.M., Hood's forces attacked part of the Army of the Cumberland just south of Peachtree Creek. The ensuing battle, which lasted until sundown, was fought largely in the open and without fortifications on either side, except for some of the Union troops who had light breastworks. Hood had hoped to catch Thomas's troops in the act of crossing Peachtree Creek, but the command system within his Army of the Tennessee was inefficient and resulted in Hood's attack taking place later than planned. Most of Thomas's troops were already well across the creek and some had already constructed breastworks. The result was a Union victory in which Hood suffered about four thousand, eight hundred casualties and Thomas only about seventeen-hundred. Hood retreated back into the fortified lines around Atlanta.

While Thomas's troops were fighting the bulk of Hood's army on the north side of Atlanta, McPherson's Army of the Tennessee continued to press closer to the city's east side, steadily driving the Confederate cavalry who were its only opposition. Already at one o'clock that afternoon some of McPherson's long-range cannon had lobbed several shells into the city. Near sundown, McPherson's men approached a prominent bald hill that seemed to be a key component of the Confederate defenses in the area, but the commander of McPherson's lead division was wounded while reconnoitering for an attack, and by the time his successor could take up the matter, darkness precluded further action. Sherman was mildly disappointed in his good friend McPherson. "I was in hopes you could make a closer approach to Atlanta," he wrote in a note to McPherson late that night. He informed McPherson of Thomas's fight that evening and expressed the hope that Hood might abandon Atlanta after the beating he had received.[5]

The next morning, McPherson attacked and took the bald hill, though hard-fighting Confederate infantry—Sherman's old Tunnel Hill nemeses of Cleburne's Division—clung grimly to a lower ridge that ran north from the hill. From the summit, McPherson's men had a clear view of Atlanta spread out in front of them. The Confederates were not content to let them stay there, however, and launched several counterattacks during the morning. The fighting was intense, but McPherson's men held on to their newly won hilltop position.[6]

During the afternoon, Union troops atop the bald hill saw columns of Confederates marching south through Atlanta—though what, if anything, such movements might mean remained a matter of conjecture. Sherman, to whom McPherson reported the observations, reckoned it meant that Hood was, as expected, pulling out of Atlanta. McPherson was less optimistic. He commented to his staff that from his knowledge of Hood when they were at West Point, he believed that the Confederate general might "lack in judgment," but he would fight at every opportunity and "with desperation." He warned his staff that they would have to take extra precautions against a surprise assault.[7]

Sherman and McPherson had contrasting concerns, and each was worried about a different potential danger. Sherman's chief worry was the possibility of the arrival of twenty-thousand Confederate troops from the Army of Northern Virginia. To guard against that danger he was anxious to destroy the Georgia Railroad—the reinforcements' most likely route of approach—thoroughly and for a long distance. The more than half dozen miles McPherson's men had torn up and burned thus far were not enough for Sherman. So to hasten and extend the process he directed Brigadier General Kenner Garrard's division of cavalry, which had been guarding McPherson's southern flank, to move to the east side of Stone Mountain and begin tearing up the rails there. McPherson's concern was quite different and related to the safety of his own command. The Army of the Tennessee was on the left of Sherman's forces, and since Sherman had removed Garrard's cavalry, its left flank was "in the air"— not anchored on any strong geographic feature and with no friendly forces beyond it. McPherson worried that Hood might attack this dangling flank. Both Sherman and McPherson hoped their fears would not be realized but that Hood would abandon Atlanta without giving battle again.[8]

Before dawn on the morning of July 22, Union skirmishers advanced and found the Confederate fortifications empty all along the line. Sherman was sure this was the anticipated evacuation of Atlanta and gave orders for all three of his armies to pursue the retreating Confederates. Before the pursuit could get started, however, the skirmishers' continued advance revealed that the Rebels had merely pulled back to an inner line of entrenchments roughly half a mile closer to Atlanta. All along the Union line, troops advanced a similar distance, took over the abandoned Confederate earthworks, and began altering them to face toward the city. In

McPherson's sector, the Army of the Tennessee's line advanced in some areas but remained anchored on the bald hill.[9]

Finding the enemy still in place that morning reawakened both Sherman's and McPherson's previous concerns. McPherson was convinced more than ever that Hood was going to attack, and he commented to his staff that he expected to fight "one of the severest battles of the campaign" that day. He ordered his reserve, Major General Grenville Dodge's Sixteenth Corps, to move to the left and take position behind his flank there, ready to counteract the assault he looked for Hood to make in that quarter. Sherman was still thinking of the Georgia Railroad as a possible conduit for suspected Confederate reinforcements from Virginia, and he wanted maximum destruction of those tracks in minimum time. Learning of McPherson's planned disposition of his reserve, Sherman fired off a dispatch to the Army of the Tennessee commander: "Instead of sending Dodge to your left, I wish you would put his whole corps at work destroying absolutely the railroad back to and including Decatur," Sherman wrote. "I want that road absolutely and completely destroyed; every tie burned and every rail twisted." He wanted this done quickly, he explained, because when it was finished, he planned to shift the Army of the Tennessee all the way around to the opposite side of Atlanta to cut the railroads there.[10]

McPherson was disturbed by these orders. He told his staff again that he expected Hood to attack his left that day, and he decided to ride over to Sherman's headquarters to discuss the matter with his commander in person. Sherman had made his headquarters in a house behind Schofield's lines near where they joined to McPherson's right. The Army of the Tennessee commander arrived at Sherman's headquarters around 11:00 A.M., and as always, the two friends greeted each other warmly. Six inches taller than the average man, handsome, and charming, the thirty-six-year-old McPherson never failed to make a good impression. Sherman had known him before the war, and they had served together throughout most of the conflict. McPherson had planned to take a leave and travel to Baltimore just before the campaign that spring to wed his fiancée, but Sherman had said the army could not spare him and talked him into waiting until after the campaign.[11]

Sherman's and McPherson's discussion of the situation was lively and cordial. The two had always worked well together. McPherson was in good spirits, pleased with the progress of the campaign, but he urged Sherman to reconsider his order. He needed the Sixteenth Corps on his flank, he explained. If the enemy had made no aggressive move by 1:00 P.M., McPherson said he would withdraw his objection to the diversion of the Sixteenth Corps to additional railroad wrecking duties. Sherman readily agreed, and the two parted cheerfully, McPherson to ride back and inspect his lines.[12]

Less than an hour later, Sherman heard firing break out in McPherson's sector and grow rapidly in intensity to what was obviously a full-scale battle. Worse, the sound seemed to extend to the rear of the Army of the Tennessee, toward Decatur. In response, Sherman had Schofield dispatch one of his brigades to Decatur to help guard the rear approaches to the Army of the Tennessee. He was pacing the veranda of his headquarters house when one of McPherson's staff officers galloped up on a lathered horse and announced that McPherson was either "killed or a prisoner." The general had ridden into a patch of woods well behind his lines, but firing had been heard—and then McPherson's riderless horse had come galloping back out of the woods, bleeding from a wound.[13]

Sherman sent orders to the Army of the Tennessee's senior corps commander, Major General John A. Logan, to assume command of the army and take the obvious steps to correct the situation: Logan was to drive out the Rebels who had somehow gotten behind the army's lines. He was then to "refuse" the army's left flank—that is, swing it back like a gate on a hinge so that the right half of the army continued to face west while the left half faced south. The hinge for the movement was to be the bald hill, which would then become the apex and key to the position.[14]

What had happened was that Hood, using two of his three corps, had launched just the sort of flank attack McPherson had anticipated. The Sixteenth Corps succeeded, as McPherson had hoped, in blunting part of the blow, but a gap between the Sixteenth and Seventeenth Corps had allowed some Confederates to penetrate the Union position and confront McPherson as he rode, well in advance of his staff, through a dense patch of woods between the two wings of his army. Summoned to surrender, McPherson wheeled his horse to ride away but was shot dead. Later in the battle, Union troops retook the ground where he fell and recovered his body. Several staff officers brought the body back to Sherman's headquarters, and he directed them to accompany their fallen chief's corpse on the long trip back to Clyde, Ohio, for burial in McPherson's hometown.[15]

Back on the battlefield outside Atlanta, the Army of the Tennessee fought on. Attacked front, flank, and rear, the army did perform the maneuver Sherman as had directed, though whether it was in response to his order or simply from the necessity of survival under heavy Confederate attack is unclear. Logan was perhaps the most inspirational personal leader of the war, with an ability to persuade almost any group of men at any time to follow anywhere he might lead. At the height of the battle, he personally led the outnumbered Army of the Tennessee troops in rallying to throw back Confederates who had briefly broken through their lines. The battle raged until nightfall, with repeated Rebel assaults on the bald hill, but the Union line ultimately held there.[16]

During the course of the battle, Sherman had Schofield mass most of the Army of the Ohio's artillery—some twenty guns—near his headquarters where they could play on the flank of the Rebels who were attacking the Army of the Tennessee. In addition, Sherman urged both Schofield and Thomas to press the Confederates in their own fronts, rightly surmising that Hood must have thinned his lines there in order to mass troops against the Army of the Tennessee. Sherman was astute in recognizing the difficulty and delay that would be involved in shifting troops from the other two armies all the way to the Army of the Tennessee's position. However, the inherent strength of the entrenched defensive meant that even the thinned Confederate defenders were still able to fend off such probes as Thomas sent against them. The Army of the Tennessee was thus left to fight Hood almost alone on July 22 and ultimately did so successfully. Union casualties from the day's fighting came to about thirty-six hundred men, while Confederate losses totaled some eighty-five hundred.[17]

The day after the battle, Sherman rode the lines of the Army of the Tennessee, pausing frequently to converse with the soldiers. The reception they gave him was enthusiastic, with regiment after regiment giving "wild cheers." A Wisconsin soldier wrote that Sherman "thanked us for the way we had conducted ourselves the day before, and lamented the death of McPherson," adding, "We thought more of him for those few words." To a young Ohio officer he gave "some useful hints," while to the staff of the Seventeenth Corps, he quipped that "the only unmilitary move that they made was not to surrender."[18]

Yet, over both Sherman and the soldiers of the Army of the Tennessee lay the pall cast by the loss of the much-loved McPherson. "This is a sad, sad day," wrote one of the victorious soldiers, while another penned, "McPherson was beloved by every soldier in his command, and there is not one but mourns the loss of so valuable a leader." To the young general's fiancée, Emily Hoffman, Sherman wrote, "I yield to none on Earth but yourself the right to excel me in lamentations for our Dead Hero."[19]

The problem remained of selecting a permanent successor to McPherson as commander of the Army of the Tennessee. Logan had taken over during the battle by reason of seniority and had done a good job. Yet Sherman rightly doubted the fiery Illinoisan's ability to handle the army consistently. If furious, straight-ahead fighting had been what Sherman planned, he could not have chosen a better general than Logan, but Sherman had not deviated from his desire to win Atlanta by maneuver rather than by attrition. "I knew that we would have to execute some most delicate maneuvers, requiring the utmost skill, nicety, and precision," Sherman later wrote, and he doubted whether Logan was equal to the task. Sherman's other top lieutenants agreed. Thomas was especially forceful in urging that the permanent command of the Army of the Tennessee go to a professional soldier rather than to Logan, who was a politician in civilian life and still thought like one. The man Sherman selected was Major General Oliver O. Howard, a West Point graduate and veteran of much hard fighting in the East, where he had lost an arm early in the war. Sherman was confident that Howard would carry out the most complicated of orders "faithfully and well."[20]

After the task of choosing a successor to McPherson came the task of mollifying or otherwise dealing with those who were not chosen, and first among them, naturally, was Logan, a fighting general whom the army needed in his position as commander of the Fifteenth Corps. "No one could have a higher appreciation of the responsibility that devolved on you so unexpectedly and the noble manner in which you met it," Sherman wrote in seeking to assuage Logan. "I fear you will be disappointed at not succeeding permanently to the command of the Army & Dept. I assure you in giving preference to Gen. Howard, I will not fail to give you every credit for having done so well. You have command of a good corps, a command that I would prefer to the more complicated one of a Dept., and if you will be patient it will come to you soon enough. Be assured of my entire confidence," Sherman concluded, signing, "Your friend." Logan stayed with the army and continued to perform well, but ever afterward he harbored a grudge against West Pointers in general and Sherman in particular. Sherman's choice of Howard over Logan was wise, and his diplomatic handling of Logan minimized its side-effects. The ill-feeling toward Sherman that Logan would cherish for years to come was unjustified but probably inevitable in a man of Logan's talent and ambition. Keeping Logan in the army, where he was all but irreplaceable as Fifteenth Corps commander—and maintaining his staunch political support for the

Union cause while home on leave a few weeks later—were both important benefits, and Sherman had done well to secure them. His skill in personal relations was one of his strengths that historians have often overlooked.[21]

Another passed-over and highly offended candidate was Joseph Hooker, commander of the Twentieth Corps within Thomas's Army of the Cumberland. Hooker was a fighting general, whom the army did not particularly need. Senior in rank to the other corps commanders of Sherman's three armies, Hooker had once commanded the prestigious Army of the Potomac, where he had demonstrated that though he was a skillful and combative corps commander, he was badly out of his depth at the next level. Thus far in the Atlanta campaign Hooker had fought hard but had repeatedly maneuvered his corps in unsafe ways in order to separate it from Thomas's army and place it alongside McPherson's or Schofield's—his juniors—so that he might get temporary command of their armies in case of action and perhaps win recognition that would make the position permanent. Howard's elevation especially galled Hooker since he had made that general the particular scapegoat for his own dismal failure at Chancellorsville, Virginia, the year before. Outraged at being passed over, Hooker asked to be relieved of his command. Thomas forwarded the request to Sherman, "approved and heartily recommended," and Sherman lost no time in carrying it out.[22]

Even while in the process of making these personnel changes, Sherman had already started his next maneuver against Atlanta. As he had told McPherson, Sherman planned to send the Army of the Tennessee all the way around from the left to the right end of his line, moving into a position on the west side of Atlanta with the goal of either cutting Confederate railroads there or at least of opening the way for the Union cavalry to range farther south and cut the vital rail lines that fed Atlanta and Hood's army. The movement began in the predawn hours of July 27, with Howard taking over the command of the Army of the Tennessee later that day while it was on the road.[23]

By dint of much hard marching, that evening the Sixteenth Corps took up a position on the right of Thomas's Army of the Cumberland, and the Seventeenth Corps marched past it to take up a position on its right. The Fifteenth Corps, heading for a position still farther to the right, had the longest march. It camped that night and continued the tramp on the morning of July 28. Sherman was riding with Howard and the Fifteenth Corps around noon that day when skirmish firing quickly escalated in front of the column. "General Hood will attack me here," Howard commented.

"I guess not," Sherman countered. "He will hardly try it again."[24]

But Howard, who had been one year behind Hood at West Point, knew the Confederate general much better than Sherman did, and he was right. For the third time in eight days, Hood had massed two of his three corps and launched a strong offensive thrust from the Atlanta lines intended to crush one component of Sherman's force. The target was once again the Army of the Tennessee, and the weight of Hood's blow, aimed at the Union flank, fell entirely on the Fifteenth Corps, which was positioned with one of its divisions facing eastward toward Atlanta and the other two facing south to guard against just such a Confederate foray. Together with Howard, Sherman quickly inspected the lines of the Fifteenth Corps, where Howard's soldiers were hastily throwing up breastworks of fence rails, tree limbs, or whatever else they could lay hands on in the few minutes that remained before the Rebels struck. Then, Sherman turned and rode back toward Thomas's sector. This was Howard's battle to fight, and Sherman would get out of his way. Sherman's leadership style allowed him to give an able subordinate room to conduct his operations in his own way. Sherman's presence with his other forces would also place him in a position to forward reinforcements quickly if they should be needed.[25]

None were. The fight, known as the Battle of Ezra Church, after a Methodist meetinghouse that stood on the battlefield, was the easiest Union victory of the campaign. The position of the Fifteenth

Corps was good, and the Confederate assaults were mostly frontal. Howard provided good leadership in his second day in army command, encouraging his men and making what few adjustments were necessary. The Rebels renewed their attacks again and again throughout the afternoon, but when the smoke had cleared, they had accomplished nothing, and their losses stood at some three-thousand men. Howard's casualties totaled little more than five hundred. Sherman was pleased to hear both of the victory and that the veterans of the Army of the Tennessee had warmly received Howard, eagerly cheering him as he walked their lines during lulls in the fighting.[26]

Despite the victories at Peachtree Creek, Atlanta, and Ezra Church, Sherman did not, as he had hoped, succeed in taking Atlanta before the end of July, or for that matter, August. He had hoped to make more out of the victory at Ezra Church, but one of Thomas's divisions that had been sent to strike the flank of the defeated Confederates could not get into position in time. As during the Battle of Atlanta, he urged Thomas and Schofield to pressure the necessarily thinned Confederate lines in their front, but they assured him that plenty of Rebels still manned the breastworks and that no progress was possible. Sherman hoped his cavalry might be able to range out and break the key railroads south and southwest of the city, but that proved to be a dismal failure. Sherman became convinced that "cavalry could not, or would not, make a sufficient lodgment on the railroad below Atlanta, and that nothing would suffice but for us to reach it with the main army." During the days and weeks that followed, he gradually stretched his lines, well protected by breastworks, until they extended some ten miles. Still, they did not reach the railroads. In that respect, he was once again in somewhat the same position he had faced at Kennesaw Mountain, with an impregnable position in front of him but yet unable to stretch his lines far enough to turn the enemy.[27]

Frustrated that he could neither assault nor, for the moment at least, turn the defenses, Sherman applied all the pressure he could, launching limited forays against Confederate skirmishers and bombarding both the defensive works and the city beyond. To do the latter more effectively, Sherman sent for a pair of long-range siege guns, "with which we can pick out almost any house in the town" and "make the inside of Atlanta too hot to be endured," he wrote to Halleck. Women and children were still inside the city of Atlanta, but that meant nothing either to Sherman or to the laws and customs of war, which held that a defended city was open to general bombardment. If Hood chose to defend the city without evacuating noncombatants, that was his problem, not Sherman's. Sherman had no intention of allowing the enemy to use his own citizens as human shields. "One thing is certain," he assured the chief-of-staff, "whether we get inside of Atlanta or not, it will be a used-up community by the time we are done with it."[28]

While the dog days passed, Union morale on the home front sagged alarmingly. Hopes had been high that spring for quick victory, but Grant was stalled in front of Richmond and Petersburg and Sherman in front of Atlanta, while the casualty lists, especially from Virginia, had been appalling. Trained military minds in both the North and South could see that Grant and Sherman had death grips on the Confederacy and would, given time, choke the life out of it, but the public and the press could see only that the war, of which they were heartily weary, was still dragging on. This was significant because 1864 was a presidential election year. The Democratic Party had nominated popular general George B. McClellan on a platform that called the war a failure and demanded negotiations—almost the only hope of survival for the hard-pressed Confederacy. Surveying the dispirited mood of the country in mid-August, America's most astute politician, Abraham Lincoln, concluded that if nothing happened to change the situation, McClellan would win the election with a mandate to seek peace without victory.

Meanwhile, back in Georgia, Sherman determined on a bold plan. He would leave only a single corps to defend the bridge over the Chattahoochee, and with the rest of his three armies he would strike out to the southwest and break those railroads. The movement began on the night of August 25, and passing to the west of Atlanta, Sherman's forces had by August 28 reached the Atlanta and West Point Railroad at Fairburn, twenty miles southwest of Atlanta, and spent the next day systematically destroying it. Then, they pressed on toward the Macon and Western. They reached it early on August 31—the Army of the Tennessee at Jonesboro, seventeen miles south of Atlanta, the Army of the Cumberland several miles closer to the city, and the Army of the Ohio still closer to Atlanta. Any one of these lodgments would have been fatal to Hood's hold on the city. As it was, the one he learned of first was that at Jonesboro. Once again, he massed two of his three corps and hurled them at Howard's Army of the Tennessee. The result was more lopsided than the Battle of Ezra Church—twenty-two-hundred Confederate killed, wounded, or missing to one hundred seventy-two of Howard's men. The next day, Sherman massed more of his forces toward Jonesboro and severely thrashed the Confederates there.

With that, Hood knew the game was finally up and ordered his troops to evacuate Atlanta after setting fires to destroy the city's military and transportation assets. In response to the noise of exploding ordnance, which sounded very much like gunfire, Major General Henry W. Slocum, commanding the Twentieth Corps at the Chattahoochee Bridge, sent reconnoitering parties toward Atlanta during the predawn hours of September 2. They found the Rebel works empty and a party of city officials coming out to meet them and transact the formal surrender of Atlanta. Slocum telegraphed Secretary of War Edwin M. Stanton, "General Sherman has taken Atlanta." Two days later, Sherman himself followed up with a dispatch to Chief-of-Staff Halleck, explaining the final operations around Atlanta and concluding, "So Atlanta is ours and fairly won."[29]

Sherman's decision to rest his troops rather than pursue Hood's army after the fall of Atlanta was to become the object of much future criticism. He may have passed up an opportunity to destroy or capture the main Rebel army in the West, although such feats were notoriously rare during the Civil War. Had Grant been in Sherman's place, he would undoubtedly have made the attempt, but in that respect Grant was simply a better general than Sherman or any other general of the Civil War. Sherman excelled in other aspects of generalship. Though he was less likely than Grant to eliminate an enemy army, Sherman was to show that he could conceive of other, less costly, ways of winning the war.

The failure to trap Hood's army after the fall of Atlanta revealed how Sherman tended to focus on different objectives than Grant did. Grant aimed at the destruction of the enemy armies, while Sherman thought in terms of taking or destroying key strategic objectives that would undercut the enemy's ability to sustain its armies. Thus, two days after the fall of Atlanta, he wrote to Halleck that there would be no point in advancing against Hood now, because "there is no valuable point to his rear till we reach Macon," and it was at present impractical to start a campaign against that city. For Grant, the object of advancing against one of the enemy's strategic points was chiefly to induce the enemy army to come out and fight, whereas for Sherman there was no reason to move against the enemy's army if not for the purpose of taking one of his strategic points. Both approaches were sensible.[30]

Sherman had also displayed weaknesses in assuming his enemy would do what Sherman hoped he would do—such as evacuating Atlanta—and in misreading his enemy's intentions—as in his failure to anticipate Hood's attacks at the battles of Atlanta and Ezra Church. In those cases, the foresight of his younger lieutenants McPherson and Howard had prevented at least a serious check to one component of Sherman's force. Throughout the war, Sherman had difficulty in calculating what the enemy was doing outside of the range of his direct observation. By this point in the conflict, however, he had learned to surround himself with such outstanding subordinates as Howard and McPherson and to listen to their concerns. Sherman had indeed come a long way since Shiloh.

The capture of Atlanta was just the sort of tangible accomplishment the Northern public needed in order to grasp that the war was not, as Democratic Party orators were telling them, a failure, but that in fact victory was on its way if only the Union remained resolute. Lincoln might perhaps have won reelection without Sherman's victory at Atlanta—though Lincoln himself thought it unlikely—but the success of the campaign did more than any other single event to insure Lincoln's victory and a reaffirmation of the North's determination to see the war through to final victory for the Union and for emancipation. In that sense, it deserves to be counted as one of the most decisive battles of the war.

Throughout the campaign, Sherman had practiced maneuver warfare more skillfully and on a wider stage than any other Civil War general had done. Only at Kennesaw Mountain had he made the mistake of attacking where Johnston wanted him to attack. On every other occasion Sherman's main effort had taken his forces around Johnston's strength to strike at vulnerable areas the Confederate general had left uncovered. Every Civil War army commander attempted to execute turning movements, but Sherman showed himself to be the master of such maneuvers. Again and again, he successfully turned his opponents, leaving them the unenviable options of retreating or fighting at a disadvantage. Johnston consistently chose retreat. Hood, just as characteristically, chose to fight. The results, ultimately, were the same. The fundamental concepts Sherman had used—maneuvering, avoiding enemy strength, capitalizing on enemy weaknesses—transcend muzzle-loading rifles and black-powder artillery and are as valid in the twenty-first century as they were in the nineteenth.

The
Atlanta
Campaign

Thomas   Schofield

McPherson

Dalton
Johnston
Tilton

Resaca
Battle of
Resaca
May 13-15

Oostanaula River

Polk

Rome   Cassville

Elowah River

Battle of
Cassville
May 19

Dallas   Marietta
New
Hope
Church

Battle of
Kennesaw
Mountain
June 27

Georgia

Battle of
Atlanta
July 20 - September 1

Chattahoochee River   Atlanta

- - - - Union Troop
Movements

———— Confederate
Troop Movements   C.Geni

CHAPTER NINE

From Atlanta to Durham Station, 1864–1865

In one sense, Sherman's capture of Atlanta, by heartening Northern voters to reelect Lincoln, had destroyed the Confederacy's last chance for survival. By giving Lincoln another four years, the Northern electorate had announced its willingness to see the war prosecuted to final victory, and by the fall of 1864, the Union clearly had the raw military might necessary to do that. Yet, that might still had to be translated into actual military operations that would finally break the will of the Confederate people to go on resisting. That task fell primarily on Grant and Sherman. Their skill would determine how and when the war would end—and how many additional lives would be lost before that time.

The obvious question after the fall of Atlanta was what Sherman's armies should do next, and that became a topic of correspondence between Grant and Sherman during the early autumn. Continuing to drive southward in the same manner Sherman had done since leaving Chattanooga that spring was impractical. Supplying his entire force via a single-track railroad for the more than one hundred miles through what had until that campaign been enemy country had been a work of logistical wizardry that represented no small part of Sherman's genius as a commander. He had made that narrow conduit haul the supplies for one hundred thousand troops, and he had defended that fragile supply line not only between Atlanta and Chattanooga but over its continuation through guerrilla-infested Tennessee and Kentucky. In all, Sherman's railroad supply line stretched four hundred miles before reaching reliably friendly territory at the Ohio River. To continue advancing with his armies dangling at the end of that tenuous ribbon of rails would have been foolhardy.

The alternatives were few. For Sherman's forces to remain stationary at Atlanta, expending their energy in maintaining their supply lines and doing occupation duty was hardly the path to victory. The choice, then, was to go forward but not by the conventional means of a carefully maintained supply line, and within days after the fall of Atlanta Sherman was contemplating such a move—to advance with a large army in a raiding mode, with no supply line at all, striking across the Deep South either to the Gulf of Mexico at Mobile or to the Atlantic at Savannah.

A few days after taking Atlanta, Sherman telegraphed Grant with his idea, and the two followed up with an exchange of letters. Several interesting targets existed in the interior of Georgia—the capital at Milledgeville, and war industries at Macon and Augusta. The Confederates could not defend them all. Sherman proposed to advance so as to present potential threats to all and then, maneuvering as usual away from the enemy's strength, do crippling damage to the Confederacy. His army could live off the land. "Where a million of people find subsistence," he wrote, echoing his statement before the Atlanta Campaign, "my army won't starve." Jauntily he concluded, "If you can whip Lee and I can march to the Atlantic I think

Uncle Abe will give us a twenty days' leave of absence to see the young folks." Grant remained uncertain. "What you are to do with the forces at your command, I do not exactly see."[1]

While he and Grant continued their exchange of thoughts in a series of letters, Sherman took action to make Atlanta a secure base for whatever further operations he might undertake. As each previous Southern city had been conquered, a division or more of Union troops had been required to garrison it, maintain order, and protect civilian life and property. The populace, often consisting largely of Confederate soldiers' families who had fled military operations in the countryside or who were otherwise without any means of support (the Confederacy was almost completely unable to pay its soldiers), soon became dependent on rations issued by the Union occupiers, who were unwilling to stand by and watch thousands of civilians starve. "These fellows," Sherman wrote, referring to Confederates soldiers in a letter to his brother-in-law, "have a way of leaving us to take care of their families." Both garrisoning cities and distributing food to Rebel dependents diminished the strength of further Union operations by reducing combat force and straining logistics.[2]

Sherman decided it would be otherwise with Atlanta. Two days after his first troops marched into the city, and before he had set foot there himself, Sherman notified Halleck that he intended to evacuate Atlanta of all nonessential civilians. Fewer garrison troops would then be needed and no extra supplies to feed the families of enemy soldiers. Removing the civilians would remove a security risk, and all the city's buildings would be available for military purposes. He would provide the evacuees with transportation north out of the war zone or else south to Confederate lines, in either case allowing them to take "clothing, trunks, reasonable furniture, bedding, etc." As to how the policy might be received, he explained to the chief-of-staff, "If the people raise a howl against my barbarity and cruelty, I will answer that war is war, and not popularity-seeking. If they want peace, they and their relatives must stop the war."[3]

The people did indeed "raise a howl," with Hood himself leading the baying. In response to a September 7 letter Sherman sent him to arrange for transportation of the refugees southward, the Confederate general fired back a missive asserting that Sherman's action "transcends, in studied and ingenious cruelty, all acts ever before brought to my attention in the dark history of war," a statement suggesting a highly limited knowledge of military history. That letter led to a heated exchange of epistles between Hood and Sherman, with Sherman demonstrating that his action was consistent with the laws of war and with the practices of Confederate commanders and also accusing Hood of hypocrisy for appealing to "God and humanity" while fighting for such a cause. Hood in turn condemned Sherman for "subjugating free white men" and helping an "inferior race."[4]

The mayor and two aldermen of Atlanta also wrote to Sherman, appealing that he rescind his order and describing at some length the hardship they believed it would entail. In reply, Sherman wrote an even longer letter that expressed much of his thought about the nature of war and the degree to which its impact on civilians could or should be limited. He admitted that some hardship would be involved in carrying out the order, but that could not be avoided. The war had to be won, and if that entailed a certain amount of suffering, so be it.

"You cannot qualify war in harsher terms than I will," Sherman wrote. "War is cruelty, and you cannot refine it." The guilt lay with the secessionists who had wrongfully started the war. "You might as well appeal against the thunderstorm as against these terrible hardships of war," he continued. "They are inevitable, and the only way the people of Atlanta can hope once more to live in peace and quiet at home, is to stop the war, which can only be done by admitting that it began in error and is perpetuated in pride." In short, Sherman believed that war was an evil brought on the people by the wicked men who had started it. The best thing good men could do—the quickest way to end the suffering—was to end the war as quickly as possible by the triumph of the cause of right. "I want peace," Sherman emphasized, "and believe it can only be reached through union and war, and I will ever conduct war with a view to perfect and early success." Then, however, when Union and peace were restored, "You may call on me for any thing. Then will I share with you the last cracker, and watch with you to shield your homes and families against danger from every quarter."[5]

For a few days in mid-September, the coming of peace seemed a little closer. A former Georgia congressman paid a call on Sherman seeking permission to recover the body of his son who had died in the Confederate army and was buried behind Union lines. The discussion turned to the war, and the Georgian agreed that the cause of the Confederacy was hopelessly lost. Sherman suggested that if he could persuade Georgia Governor Joseph Brown to withdraw Georgia and Georgia's troops from the Confederacy, he, Sherman, would guarantee that in whatever future advances he would make into Georgia his army would keep to the roads, doing no foraging and acquiring local goods only by purchase. Subsequently, he gave the same message to other Georgia politicians who he hoped might serve as intermediaries. Sherman kept Washington well apprised of the venture and Lincoln showed a strong interest. Brown did not. The Georgia governor was a thorn in the side of Jefferson Davis, but he was not ready to quit the Confederacy. So the war would go on, and Georgia would feel its scourge along with the rest of the South.[6]

A few days later, Sherman became aware that Hood was gradually shifting his army to the west, toward the Alabama line. One did not have to be a clairvoyant to predict that the Confederate general planned to go around Atlanta and try to threaten Sherman's supply line in northern Georgia, thus forcing Sherman to abandon Atlanta and any thought of further offensive operations and devote himself to trying to chase Hood off of his railroad. Sherman was at once disinclined to play that game. On September 25 he telegraphed Halleck, "If I were sure that Savannah would soon be in our possession, I should be tempted to march for Milledgeville and Augusta; but," he conceded, "I must first secure what I have." Writing in his memoirs, twenty years later, Sherman would say that it was at this point that the concept of the coming campaign first entered his "'mind's eye.'" For now, though, Grant too felt it would be better for Sherman to secure his supply lines before going south.[7]

Several days later, Sherman learned that Jefferson Davis was on a visit to Hood and had been passing through the Confederate-held portions of Georgia making speeches, duly reported in newspapers that Sherman was soon perusing with intense interest. Davis boasted that Hood would move north and cut Sherman's supply lines, forcing a Union retreat that would be more disastrous than that of Napoleon from Moscow. Davis's speech made Sherman all the more certain as to what he wanted to do next with his army, but he continued to be unsure as to exactly how and when. For the present, however, Sherman responded to the threat by detaching three divisions of his force to northern Georgia and Tennessee and sending George Thomas to command them along with the large number of additional Union forces that had already been guarding the railroad. On October 3, Sherman learned that Hood was aiming to strike the Western and Atlantic somewhere in the neighborhood of Marietta or Kingston, Georgia, and he reacted immediately by leaving the Twentieth Corps to hold Atlanta and the Chattahoochee bridges while with the rest of his forces he marched north to intercept Hood.[8]

They reached Marietta on October 4, but Hood's army was not there. The Rebels had cut the telegraph wires leading north, so that Sherman's only clue to Hood's whereabouts and activity was a report that Union scouts atop Kennesaw had spotted Confederate columns on the far side of the mountain marching north. Sherman guessed Hood was aiming for the large Union supply depot at Allatoona Pass, guarded by a small brigade. Over the heads of the Rebels on the plain below, Sherman's signalmen used flag semaphore and notified Brigadier General John M. Corse to take his division from Rome to Allatoona to reinforce the garrison there. It was difficult to say whether Corse, forty miles away, would receive the message in time to reach Allatoona.[9]

Sherman himself reached the summit of Kennesaw the next morning and in fine weather surveyed an impressive panorama. Extending north from the foot of the mountain, the Rebels had destroyed eight miles of railroad, from Big Shanty to Acworth, and the smoke from the piles of burning ties rose in the clear morning air. Farther away, some eighteen miles from Kennesaw, white clouds of powder smoke rose from Allatoona, where the rumble of cannon indicated a battle was raging. After a long, tense wait, the signalman on Kennesaw made out the distant wig-wag of his counterpart's flag inside the Allatoona fortifications signaling "Corse is here." That was a relief to Sherman, who had not previously been sure that Corse had received his message.

The battle continued through most of the day, while Sherman gauged the progress of his army on its way to relieve Corse by smoke signals his officers sent up periodically from the head of the column. Finally, around 4:00 P.M. the fighting at Allatoona ended, and subsequent messages indicated Corse had held the fort, despite being able to get little more than a single brigade of his division to Allatoona before the Rebels struck. Sherman detailed ten thousand men to work on repairing the railroad, and along with the regular repair crews, they had it running again within a week.[10]

Sherman had thus turned aside Hood's blow at his communications, but he was more eager than ever to cease playing this game of chasing Hood through the mountains. Indeed, he would later say that by this time, he "had no longer a shadow of doubt" what his next campaign should be. Already, on October 1, he had telegraphed his thoughts to Grant. "Why will it not do to leave Tennessee to the forces which Thomas has, and the reserves soon to come to Nashville, and for me to destroy Atlanta and march across Georgia to Savannah or Charleston, breaking roads and doing irreparable damage?" He added, "We cannot remain on the defensive." On October 9, from Allatoona, which he had reached just that day, Sherman wrote Grant, pointing out the futility of trying to keep Rebel raiders off his railroad and advocating a massive raid through Georgia.

"Until we can repopulate Georgia," Sherman wrote, "it is useless to occupy it, but the utter destruction of its roads, houses, and people will cripple their military resources. By attempting to hold the roads we will lose 1,000 men monthly, and will gain no result." With the confidence that had become typical of him at this point in the war, he concluded, "I can make the march, and make Georgia howl." The next day he telegraphed Grant again pleading the same cause.[11]

Grant remained skeptical. In a telegram the following day, he expressed concern that Hood would ignore Sherman and go north into Tennessee, probably heading for Nashville, confident he could damage the Union more there than Sherman could hurt the Confederacy in Georgia, and Grant did not believe Thomas would be able to stop him. True to form, Grant added, "If there is any way of getting at Hood's army I would prefer that." Grant would always think in terms of destroying the enemy armies before taking the enemy's strategic points.[12]

Sherman stuck to his guns. "We cannot remain here on the defensive," he telegraphed back to Grant that same October 11. Hood could always find a way to break the railroad, and all Sherman would be able to do was chase him ineffectually. Again he urged Grant to let him "move through Georgia, smashing things to the sea." If Grant let him go south, he explained, then "instead of my being on the defensive, I would be on the offensive; instead of guessing at what he means to do, he would have to guess at my plans. The difference in war," Sherman concluded, "is full 25 per cent," and he added an assurance: "I can make Savannah, Charleston, or the mouth of the Chattahoochee." At 11:30 that night Grant sent his reluctant reply. "If you are satisfied the trip to the sea-coast can be made, holding the line of the Tennessee River firmly, you may make it, destroying all the railroad south of Dalton or Chattanooga, as you think best."[13]

Sherman did not believe Thomas could hold the line of the Tennessee River, keeping Hood completely out of the state of Tennessee, but he did believe Thomas could deal successfully with the Rebel once he got there. He did not, therefore, consider Grant's late-night October 11 dispatch as the permission he needed. That came in a dispatch from Halleck, which Sherman received at Ship's Gap, Georgia, on October 15, when he was still chasing Hood.

True to his word, Grant had written Secretary of War Edwin M. Stanton on October 13, "On mature reflection, I believe Sherman's proposition is the best that can be adopted." Grant had come around to Sherman's view that a continued defensive effort to keep Hood off his communications was futile. Thomas would be able to deal with Hood, and as for the danger that Sherman's army might be cut off, Grant concluded, "Such an army as Sherman has (and with such a commander) is hard to corner or capture." That same day Grant had sent orders to Halleck to have provision ships dispatched to the southern coast, ready to meet Sherman's army when it reached Savannah. Both Stanton and Halleck forwarded the dispatches to Sherman, and it was these he received at Ship's Gap.[14]

Sherman immediately began his preparations. He ordered the Fourth and Twenty-third Corps to join Thomas for the defense of Tennessee. His remaining troops, the Fifteenth and Seventeenth Corps under Howard, and the Fourteenth and Twentieth Corps, now under Slocum, he ordered to send to the rear all sick men, weak horses, rickety wagons, and excess baggage. Getting the troops to Atlanta, accumulating supplies, preparing two pontoon trains, and otherwise making ready for a long, strenuous, and potentially dangerous campaign occupied the rest of the month of October. On the last day of the month, contemplating the coming operation, Sherman told a staff officer, "It's a big game, but I can do it—I *know* I can do it."[15]

While Sherman was preparing for the campaign into Georgia, Hood was embarking on a campaign of his own—one that threatened the cancellation of the orders Sherman had worked so hard to obtain. Swinging west and then north to Florence on the Tennessee River in Alabama, Hood was obviously in the process of making just the sort of campaign Grant had anticipated, and the Rebel general could be expected to march soon toward Nashville. Disturbed by Hood's unopposed advance to the Tennessee, Grant telegraphed Sherman on the evening of November 1, "Do you not think it advisable, now that Hood has gone so far north, to entirely settle him before starting on your proposed campaign?" With typical Grantian thinking, the general-in-chief continued, "With Hood's army destroyed you can go where you please with impunity." After adding several more arguments Grant concluded, "If you can see a chance of destroying Hood's army, attend to that first, and make your other move secondary."[16]

Sherman responded the next day in three separate telegraph dispatches to Grant. Repeatedly, he pressed his by now familiar points. Thomas was well able to handle Hood if the latter advanced into Tennessee. "No single army can catch Hood" by chasing him. Sherman would be wasting his time in doing so, and he would also be fulfilling "Jeff Davis's cherished plan of making me leave Georgia by maneuvering." Sherman, who had advanced all the way to Atlanta by skillful maneuvering, was almost viscerally unwilling to have the same methods used successfully on him. He would not, when turned, react either as Johnston had done, by retreating, or as Hood had done, in attacking. Instead, he would answer with an even more daring maneuver: to slice deep into the enemy's vitals. "If I turn back, the whole effect of my campaign will be lost," Sherman concluded forcefully. "I am clearly of opinion that the best results will follow my contemplated movement through Georgia."[17]

Sherman's arguments were more than enough to persuade Grant. After the first of Sherman's three November 2 dispatches, the general-in-chief relented. Thomas should indeed have more than enough force to "take care of Hood and destroy him," Grant allowed. As for Sherman's main force, Grant opined, "I do not see that you can withdraw from where you are to follow Hood, without giving up all we have gained in territory. I say, then, go on as you propose."[18]

Sherman's preparations went on apace, and by November 6, he could telegraph Grant that his arrangements were nearly complete and that he would be ready to march as soon as the national elections had been held among his troops. He set November 10 as the day for the operation to begin. Back from Grant the next day came a message that underscored the strength of the relationship that had carried the two men through the recent disagreement about operations. "Great good fortune attend you!" Grant wrote. "I believe you will be eminently successful, and, at worst, can only make a march less fruitful of results than hoped for."[19]

True to his word, on November 10, Sherman set in motion the operation that was to become known as the March to the Sea. The first step was vacating and desolating the territory between Chattanooga and Atlanta. On the tenth, Sherman ordered Corse to burn Rome's mills, foundries, and factories. The next day, while moving down to Atlanta with his troops, Sherman exchanged final telegraph communications with Thomas at Nashville just before his men destroyed the lines. Pressing on, Sherman and his men passed the last trains of Union rear-area personnel heading back up the tracks to Chattanooga. Then his men tore up the rails.

Riding on toward Atlanta alongside the marching column, Sherman reflected on the curious state of affairs. "It surely was a strange event—two hostile armies marching in opposite directions, each in the full belief that it was achieving a final and conclusive result in a great war." For himself, though, Sherman was "strongly inspired with the feeling that the movement on our part was a direct attack upon the rebel army and the rebel capital at Richmond, though a full thousand miles of hostile country intervened, and that, for better or worse, it would end the war." As he had through the Atlanta Campaign, but now on a vastly larger scale, Sherman was striking to break the enemy's strength without sending his troops directly against enemy strong points.[20]

The troops continued toward Atlanta, destroying the railroad as they went, and by November 15, had reached the city, where Sherman's engineers had already been hard at work neutralizing Atlanta as a potential future base for Confederate operations. That night saw the climax of their efforts. At dinner Sherman remarked, "We have been fighting *Atlanta* all the time, in the past: have been capturing guns, wagons, etc., etc., marked '*Atlanta*' and made here, all the time: and now since they have been doing so much to destroy us and our Government we have to destroy them, at least enough to prevent any more of that."[21]

Sherman's orders called for the destruction of "railroad track, depots, car and store houses, shops, and indeed everything that might be used to our disadvantage by an enemy." His men burned the railroad depot—Atlanta's great four-hundred-foot-long brick Car Shed—as well as the roundhouse, and the railroad machine shops. At the same time, Sherman gave strict orders for posting sentries at other structures, including several church buildings, to insure that overenthusiastic soldiers did not put the torch to them as well. The Confederates had been storing ammunition in one of the buildings earmarked for destruction, and when the flames reached the explosives, the detonations hurled fragments almost to the house where Sherman was staying. The explosions spread the fires to a block of stores near the depot, but the residential areas of the city remained for the most part unscathed.[22]

The last of Sherman's troops tramped out of Atlanta the next morning, November 16, and the March to the Sea was under way. Sherman himself left town with his staff around 7:00 A.M., riding through the still smoking district that had been burned the evening before. They passed on over the July 22 battlefield, and Sherman noticed the copse of woods where McPherson fell. Major Henry Hitchcock, a recent addition to Sherman's staff, thought his chief quiet and thoughtful that morning. A regimental band struck up the John Brown song, and the soldiers joined in, singing lustily, "John Brown's body lies a moldering in the grave, his soul goes marching on." Sherman thought he had never "heard the chorus of 'Glory, glory, hallelujah!' done with more spirit, or in better harmony of time and place," as behind the marching column, as smoke continued to rise from Atlanta. The troops were in an exuberant mood, striding along energetically, and as Sherman passed, now and then a man would call out, using their affectionate nickname for their commanding general, "Uncle Billy, I guess Grant is waiting for us at Richmond!" Many thought they were bound for Richmond but none particularly cared where they were bound, as long as Uncle Billy was directing them.[23]

If the destination of the march was hard to guess, that was exactly the way Sherman wanted it. His army was divided into two columns. The one with which he and his staff were riding during the first part of the march was Major General Henry W. Slocum's, soon to be called the Army of Georgia, composed of the Fourteenth and Twentieth Corps. It marched east through Decatur and then swung southeast on a route that seemed to threaten the cluster of Confederate war industries at Augusta, Georgia. The other column was Major General Oliver O. Howard's Army of the Tennessee, composed of the Fifteenth and Seventeenth Corps, which had marched south out of Atlanta on a heading that seemed to bode ill for the equally important manufacturing center of Macon, Georgia, before veering southeastward to parallel and then gradually converge with Slocum's column. The Confederates, with their scant defensive forces consisting of cavalry and militia, divided their strength in an attempt to cover both cities, and then Sherman's columns plunged between them and passed with no contact at all save for a minor brush between a brigade of Howard's troops and a large division of Georgia militia at Griswoldville, not far from Macon, on November 22. Howard's veterans won a lopsided victory over their more numerous but woefully inexperienced assailants.

Though confident of his army's ability to whip any remotely comparable Rebel force—and confident that the Confederates could bring no such force to bear on him—Sherman nevertheless knew that it was important to minimize the resistance he encountered on the march. He had carefully studied the data of the 1860 census and had planned his route to lead through the most agriculturally rich counties in Georgia. His army would have no trouble feeding itself from the countryside provided it could stay moving and keep spread out, constantly sweeping supplies out of large new swaths of territory. Even a weak enemy force could create dangerous problems by obstructing the army's path, contesting river crossings, and forcing Sherman to concentrate his forces so that they could not gather adequate supplies. After the march was over, the impression developed that Sherman could have taken his army anywhere he wished in the heartland of the Confederacy with complete impunity. He might have, but in reality he planned his maneuver carefully so as to avoid the enemy's areas of strength, such as they were, and strike where he could do the most damage at the least cost.

Sherman had given his troops orders to "forage liberally on the country" during the march, but this did not mean he intended or would allow his men to run amuck all the way from Atlanta to Savannah. His orders specified that foraging at any significant distance from the line of march would be carried out by foraging parties regularly detailed from each brigade and led by officers. The rest of the troops could gather nearby food during halts on the march, but soldiers were not to enter houses. Only the corps commanders had the authority to order the burning of private buildings such as houses, barns, cotton gins, and the like, and Sherman advised them to do so only in response to local resistance. Public buildings, factories, warehouses, depots, and anything related to a railroad were of course marked for destruction. Draft animals of every sort were fair game for taking, but Sherman admonished his men to discriminate as to which citizens they thus relieved of livestock "between the rich, who are usually hostile, and the poor and industrious, usually neutral or friendly." All foragers were to refrain from "abusive or threatening language" and were to "endeavor to leave with each family a reasonable portion for their maintenance."[24]

The army carried out these orders substantially though not perfectly. Major Hitchcock noted that it was the fifth day of the march before he saw a single private structure burned, and that was a cotton gin probably ignited by stragglers. Extensive straggling was the largest area of violation of Sherman's order for the march, despite the vigorous efforts of the various generals. Some soldiers wandered off to forage on their own, looking for adventure and better fare. In later years such unauthorized, individual foragers would come to be called *bummers*. During the campaign, they were still usually referred to as simply foragers. In any case, the majority of Sherman's troops stayed in the ranks during marches.

The bummers operated outside of the view or the control of officers, frequently entered houses, and sometimes took items other than food, though plundering of nonfood items was limited by the practical difficulties of transporting booty over the three hundred-mile route to the sea. Few soldiers would have wanted to carry much extra weight of loot on their backs over that distance. To the extent that violations of Sherman's orders occurred, they were usually the work of the bummers. In his diary, Hitchcock, who had recently transitioned from civilian life, fretted about the bummers and their destruction, noting, "Certainly an army is a terrible engine and hard to control." Still, having made careful inquiries, he could learn of no case of a civilian suffering any physical violence from one of Sherman's soldiers.[25]

The civilians knew what to expect from Sherman and his men. Though most of the men along the line of march hid out or fled the area, taking as much livestock with them as they could and fearing that the Federals would make them all prisoners of war, the women-folk stayed home to meet the invaders, showing little fear. They clearly understood that civilians, particularly women, were untouchable unless they committed overtly hostile acts.[26]

For all of his tough talk about how the South would have to suffer for its rebellion, Sherman did not enjoy seeing that suffering. One day as the column was passing a farm, the soldiers fell out of ranks and quickly began gathering up every pig, chicken, and cow on the place, as well as all the fodder. An old woman who was mistress of the premises, seeing Sherman riding by, ran out to the gate and begged him to post a guard to prevent the plundering of her livestock and supplies. Sherman answered, "not roughly but firmly," that he could not do that. The army was moving and could not afford to post guards at every farm it passed. That night as he sat with Major Hitchcock at the campfire, he mused, "I'll have to harden my heart to these things. That poor woman today—how could I help her? There's no help for it. The soldiers will take all she has. Jeff Davis is responsible for all this." He saw the necessity as well as the justness of hard measures, but they pained him nonetheless.[27]

Some destruction was much easier for Sherman to stomach. On a cold blustery November 22, his headquarters party took shelter at a plantation north of Milledgeville, only to learn that the plantation belonged to Howell Cobb, a prominent Georgia politician and secessionist who had served in the Confederate army and in Jefferson Davis's cabinet. Sherman gave orders that as soon as his party vacated the place, his men were to destroy the entire premises with the exception of the slave quarters, and even the normally squeamish Hitchcock felt well satisfied with that outcome.[28]

One class of Georgians was delighted with the approach of Sherman's army. African-Americans hailed the arrival of the troops with jubilation. Sherman frequently sought out these blacks, especially older ones, for conversation, both to gain information about any possible Confederate efforts to impede the march and out of curiosity about the soon-to-be-freed slaves and their understanding of the war. He found that they had a remarkably clear grasp of the reasons for the war and its impending result in their own freedom. He urged the blacks to remain in their current homes and not to follow the army. Vigorous young men could join up as teamsters or members of the pioneer corps, but the army could provide neither food, nor transportation, or protection for families, children, the aged, or infirm. Their presence with the army would endanger both it and themselves. Union victory would assure their freedom. Some of them heeded his advice, but enough did not, and they created a long tail of contrabands streaming along behind the army, often experiencing the hardships of which Sherman had warned.[29]

Sherman's troops entered Milledgeville, the capital of Georgia, on November 23, sparing the statehouse but destroying as usual any structures that had been used in the Confederate war effort and continuing the steady destruction of mile after mile of railroad track. With the exception of the affair at Griswoldville that same day and the constant but ineffectual harassment of Confederate cavalry, the march met no resistance, leading Sherman to remark to Hitchcock, "Pierce the shell of the C.S.A., and it's all hollow inside."[30]

The march passed on from the rich agricultural district of middle Georgia into the more sparsely settled and less productive lands of the wiregrass and piney woods regions. The soldiers fared less sumptuously than heretofore, but the army was never close to starvation. Food continued to be relatively scarce as they approached Savannah, and increasingly the countryside did yield such food as rice, nourishing enough, to be sure, but monotonous and unfamiliar to Sherman's Midwestern soldiers.

When they reached Millen on December 3, eighty-five miles from Savannah, Sherman was riding with Howard's column. Near Millen was the site of a Confederate prisoner of war camp, and Sherman had hoped to liberate the prisoners there, but the Confederates alertly moved their prisoners two days before Sherman's arrival. The conditions at the camp, as well as the many graves and several unburied bodies emaciated to skeletal proportions, infuriated Sherman's troops and made the task of burning the large Confederate supply depot at Millen all the more enjoyable. A few soldiers surreptitiously added a nearby hotel to the conflagration.[31]

Nine miles from Savannah, Sherman and his staff came upon a column of the Seventeenth Corps that had left the road and was marching along through the fields next to it. A group of men were standing around a fence corner, where Sherman upon arriving found an officer whose foot had been blown off by a land mine, or, in the parlance of that day, a *torpedo*. The Confederates had mined this stretch of road in anticipation of Sherman's approach, burying in the sandy soil artillery shells rigged to go off when stepped on. Just then a squad of Confederate prisoners of war arrived under guard, ordered up by Seventeenth Corps commander Major General Frank Blair. The consensus of thought on the Union side was that the use of land mines away from fortifications and without other indications of their presence was a violation of the laws and customs of war. Blair had therefore ordered his provost guard detail to bring the prisoners forward and have them clear the road in front of his corps. Sherman listened to the various officers' reports of the incident. "This was not war, but murder," he concluded, "and it made me very angry." He grimly approved Blair's proposed solution. The prisoners were horrified, and two of them "begged . . . very hard to be let off." Sherman was implacable. As Hitchcock recorded the exchange in his diary that night, Sherman "told them their people had put these things there to assassinate our men instead of fighting them fair, and they must remove them; and if *they* got blown up he didn't care." The fastidious Hitchcock, a lawyer in civilian life, enthusiastically approved. "He did exactly right."[32]

Arriving in front of Savannah, Sherman found the city protected by well-built fortifications manned by Confederate troops. Once again, he declined to order a direct assault and decided instead to lay siege to the city. In order to do so, his first requirement was to make contact with Union naval forces hovering offshore and open a supply line to feed his men, who were already tiring of a steady diet of rice. The best route to the sea was via the Ogeechee River and Ossabaw Sound, south of Savannah. Blocking that route was a Confederate earthwork known as Fort McAllister, and Sherman immediately issued orders for the nearest Union column—Howard's—to take the fort. Howard assigned the assault to the division of Brigadier General William B. Hazen, which had been Sherman's own division at Shiloh. In order to observe the assault, Sherman, Howard, and their staffs, took position at an old rice mill lying on the far side of the Ogeechee, and some associated tidal marshes.

About an hour before sundown, as Sherman and the others waited for Hazen to get into position, they saw a steamer approach through Ossabaw Sound and soon could make out the stars and stripes flying from its halyards. It was the tug *Dandelion,* of Admiral John A. Dahlgren's blockading squadron. An army signal team on the tug contacted Sherman's signalmen by wig-wag: "Who are you?"

"General Sherman," was the reply.

"Is Fort McAllister taken?" the *Dandelion* wanted to know, and Sherman's signalmen replied, "Not yet, but it will be in a minute." They were almost right. Moments after the signaled exchange, Hazen's troops charged and, after a sharp fifteen minutes of fighting, took the fort. That night and the following day, Sherman went aboard a U.S. navy vessel in Ossabaw Sound and conferred with Admiral Dahlgren and with Major General John G. Foster, who commanded Union army forces along the southern coast. Supply ships that had been standing by began off-loading their cargoes, and Sherman's soldiers were soon enjoying their accustomed hardtack and salt pork—eked out by whatever they could acquire locally.[33]

With Sherman's army supplied by sea, the fall of Savannah was a matter of time. Knowing this, Confederate garrison commander Lieutenant General William J. Hardee took advantage of the opportunity to evacuate his troops through the swamps and across the Savannah River to South Carolina before Sherman could close off this avenue of escape. Once again, some would criticize Sherman for allowing an enemy army to escape, but what he had won amounted to much more. Sherman's troops marched into Savannah on December 21, and the follow morning he telegraphed Lincoln: "I beg to present you, as a Christmas gift, the city of Savannah, with 150 heavy guns and plenty of ammunition, and also about 25,000 bales of cotton."[34]

Back in contact with the outside world again, Sherman once more took up with Grant the discussion of what military operation should come next. Thomas had, only a few days before, soundly thrashed Hood at Nashville, securing Tennessee and opening the way for Union incursion into Alabama. With Sherman's army clearly no longer needed in the by now thoroughly conquered western theater, Grant directed him to bring it to Virginia by sea to join him in finishing off Lee and winning the war. Sherman was more than ready to come to Virginia, but he did not wish to travel by sea. It would take too long to assemble the necessarily large number of ships, and sea transport would dull the fine edge to which Sherman believed he had honed his army. Instead, he urged Grant to let him march through the Carolinas as he had through Georgia. "I feel confident that I can break up the whole railroad system of South Carolina and North Carolina," Sherman wrote, adding that he could have his army poised on the southern border of Virginia in time for the opening of the spring campaign. Grant readily agreed, and Sherman eagerly prepared for his next great campaign.[35]

The Carolinas Campaign, which began February 1, 1865, posed much larger challenges than had the March to the Sea. Whereas the march through Georgia had traveled mostly parallel to the rivers, that across the Carolinas would be squarely athwart every one of them. The March to the Sea had been carried out in mostly good weather, but winter in the Carolinas promised nearly constant rain, swelling the low country's creeks to torrents and vastly enlarging its swamps. The march through Georgia had been unopposed by any significant Confederate force, but in the Carolinas, Sherman would have to contend with General Joseph E. Johnston, restored to command and leading a force composed of the remnants of Hood's old army.

It was an amazing testament to Sherman's skill and that of his troops that they carried out the campaign with the same seemingly effortless ease as they had through Georgia. They waded miles of swamps, sometimes under enemy fire—Sherman sometimes wading with them. They corduroyed scores of miles of muddy roads. When Johnston did venture to meet them, at Bentonville, North Carolina, they soundly thrashed him, and had Sherman possessed Grant's knack for closing the deal, he might well have bagged Johnston's entire badly outnumbered army. Despite the harassment of Confederate cavalry, Sherman's energetic foragers and ubiquitous bummers continued to sweep plenty of food from the surrounding countryside so that the army never went hungry.

One of the campaign's more notorious incidents came on February 17 when Sherman's troops took Columbia, South Carolina. That night about a third of the city burned in a series of fires of uncertain origin. South Carolinians and other Southerners ever afterward blamed the brute Sherman and his vandals for the mishap, though at least some of the fires were no doubt started by retreating Confederates the day before, who in their misguided zeal had stacked cotton bales in the streets and then set fire to them to keep them from falling into the hands of Sherman's troops—who would have burned them anyway. Other fires may have been started by escaped Union prisoners of war, former slaves, and escaped inmates of the city jail—all of whom were known to have been at large in the city that night. Some of the fires, no doubt, were the work of Sherman's men, many of whom were eager to see the birthplace of secession go up in flames, and the whole conflagration was boosted by a fierce wind that blew most of the night. Sherman had not ordered or desired the city's burning, but he would lose no sleep over it.[36]

During the latter stages of the campaign, Sherman had to deal with the question of enemy atrocities. Even during the campaign in Georgia, some of Sherman's cavalrymen had been murdered after being captured. During the Carolinas Campaign, the practice became far more widespread with both cavalry and infantry foragers as the victims. On a number of occasions, Sherman's columns came on the corpses of small groups of their comrades, hanged or with throats cut, sometimes with crudely lettered signs attached to their clothes promising death to all foragers. Foraging was well within the laws and customs of war. Murdering prisoners was not. Sherman sent a note under flag of truce to Confederate cavalry commander Wade Hampton, but Hampton responded that he was going to go right on murdering Sherman's men every chance he got.

Sherman saw no alternative for protecting his men other than to institute a policy of strict retaliation. Such a policy was relatively easy to implement on the rare occasions when Union troops quickly caught the likely perpetrators or at least members of their unit. When it meant forcing Confederate prisoners to draw lots and then shooting the loser in cold blood, it proved to be almost more than Sherman's hardened veterans could stomach. They implemented it in one case only, when to everyone's horror, the victim turned out to be a middle-aged family man. Thereafter, no one saw fit to order retaliation again. Hampton went right on murdering prisoners, and even as Sherman and Johnston were arranging a place to meet and negotiate the latter's surrender, Hampton's troops murdered two and left a third for dead. Hampton lived another thirty-seven years, serving as a white-supremacist terrorist leader, governor, and U.S. senator, and dying peacefully in bed at the age of eighty-four, subsequently to be honored with a statue on the South Carolina capitol grounds and in the naming of various streets in that state and elsewhere.

The end of the war for Sherman and his men came in April. On the fourteenth of that month, Johnston proposed negotiations, and four days later at Durham Station, North Carolina, he and Sherman agreed on a far-reaching peace agreement—too far-reaching, as it turned out. Sherman had misunderstood Lincoln's desire for a magnanimous peace, allowing his own inherent sympathy for the South to overcome his good judgment once the prospect of a cessation of hostilities loomed. The agreement he signed seemed to imply recognition of the rebellious Confederate state governments and allowed Rebel armies to store their weapons in their state capitals and disband as if they had not been waging bloody war on the United States for four years. To make matters worse, Sherman's announcement of the terms arrived in Washington a few days after Lincoln's assassination, prompting the choleric and not overly stable Secretary of War Edwin M. Stanton to say a number of intemperate things about Sherman, just short of accusing him of outright treason. Stanton ordered Grant to travel to North Carolina and take over from Sherman. Grant went, but tactfully left Sherman in command and allowed him to renegotiate a more modest agreement with Johnston based on the terms Grant had recently accorded to Robert E. Lee's surrendering army in Virginia.

By the end of the Civil War, Sherman and Grant had formed one of the most successful collaborations in military history; yet they had fundamentally different approaches to war, and each of these approaches played an important role in the Union victory. While Grant took a Napoleonic view that saw the enemy's armies as his center of gravity, Sherman looked beyond the enemy's armies to deep penetration of his territory, destroying communications, transportation, and the means of supplying and equipping the armies in the field. His marches also served to demoralize the enemy, not so much by any damage his troops may have done—much exaggerated in legend—as by their mere presence. If many Confederate soldiers were fighting simply to keep the Yankees out of their home counties, news that Sherman had visited their homes removed that motivation. It was not what Sherman's troops did but simply that they were there.

With the conclusion of the Civil War, Sherman enjoyed enormous nationwide popularity. Second only to Grant, he was the most admired and trusted man in America. His future career would be one of high rank in the postwar army.

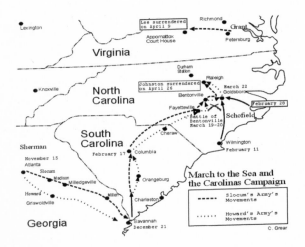

Lexington

Richmond
Lee surrendered
on April 9   ←---- Grant
Appomattox   Petersburg
Court House

Virginia

Durham
Station
Raleigh
Johnston surrendered   March 22
on April 26   Goldsboro
Bentonville
February 20

Knoxville

North
Carolina

Fayetteville
Battle of   Schofield
Bentonville
March 19-20

Cheraw

South
Carolina   Wilmington
February 11

February 17   Columbia

Sherman

November 15   Orangeburg   March to the Sea and
Atlanta   the Carolinas Campaign
Slocum
Madison   ------ Slocum's Army's
Milledgeville   Movements
Howard   Miller
Griswoldville   Charleston   .... Howard's Army's
                                              Movements

Georgia   Savannah
December 21   C. Grear

CHAPTER TEN

From Durham Station
to St. Louis, 1865–1891

IN THE WAKE OF VICTORY, THE NATION SHOWERED SHERMAN with accolades and more tangible expressions of gratitude. The citizens of Ohio started raising funds for a testimonial gift and netted $10,000 before the year was out. When Sherman was posted to St. Louis and moved his family there, the people of that city presented him with a house and a $5,000 cash gift. There and elsewhere Sherman was the honored guest at various banquets, fetes, and receptions—serenaded and celebrated from one end of the country to the other. In the early years, before legend replaced memory as a source of knowledge about the war, he was even admired in the South.[1]

The posting to St. Louis was Grant's doing, and it was exactly what Sherman wanted. He loathed politicians almost as much as he did newspapermen, and he desperately wanted to stay clear of

Washington and the roiling political battles of Reconstruction. Knowing his friend's wishes, Grant assigned Sherman to the Military Division of the Missouri, headquartered in St. Louis and comprising the vast expanse of country west of the Mississippi all the way to the Rocky Mountains, with the exception of Texas. Sherman loved it. It was far from Washington and in the West, which had always appealed strongly to him.[2]

Sherman's chief official challenge in his new assignment was in dealing with Indians, who were irate that changing times were bringing a close to the way of life they had long practiced on the plains. Sherman strongly disapproved of the Indians' aversion to common labor, their lack of an ordered society, and their inefficient use of the land. They needed to learn to live as whites did or at least to remain on their reservations. "Sooner or later," he wrote, "these Sioux will have to be wiped out or made to stay just where they are put." He favored a forceful policy to crush Indian resistance, but urged his officers at the same time to maintain "a due regard to humanity and mercy." Noting that the Ute Indians' only acts of hostility were stealing occasional sheep when compelled by hunger, Sherman refused to pursue their extinction as some clamored for him to do. "I will not permit them to be warred on," he insisted.[3]

Sherman had to direct operations on the Great Plains with an inadequate and steadily diminishing army. From a million men at the end of the war, the army shrank over the course of the next decade to about twenty-five thousand men, a fair proportion of whom were stationed in the former Confederate states as occupation troops until 1876. Sherman frequently warned that troop strength was too low, and occasional mishaps on the frontier, such as the December 1866 Fetterman Massacre, bore him out.[4]

Ever since his days in California during the 1850s, Sherman had been a warm supporter of the idea of a transcontinental railroad linking California to the rest of the United States. He strongly supported his old Army of the Tennessee comrade and Sixteenth Corps commander Grenville Dodge for the job of chief engineer on the construction of the Union Pacific Railroad, pushing the tracks westward from Council Bluffs, Iowa, toward a junction with the Central Pacific, coming the other way, somewhere in the intermontane region of the West. Sherman gave the project all the support he could, taking steps to keep hostile Indians from interfering with construction from its beginnings in 1866 until the driving of the last spike at Promontory Summit, Utah, three years later. In his honor, the makers of the railroad placed his name on the highest point on the entire line, eight thousand two hundred forty-two foot Sherman Summit, in the Laramie Mountains west of Cheyenne, Wyoming. A decade and a half after the road was completed, Sherman referred to the entire project of the transcontinental railroad as "one of the greatest and most beneficent achievements of man on earth."[5]

While Sherman backed the transcontinental railroad and struggled against the Indians on the plains during the late 1860s, he also struggled to avoid being drawn into the vortex of Reconstruction politics in Washington. In that effort, his own political naïveté and propensity for speaking his mind were sometimes his worst enemies. He had by this time come around to the view of applauding the end of slavery. He wanted the former slaves to receive humane treatment, but he did not want them to have the vote, and he did not see how unlikely they were to have one without the other. In keeping with his long-standing sympathy for Southern whites and his recent effort to make an excessively lenient peace agreement with armed Rebels, Sherman cordially approved of President Andrew Johnson's policy of a minimal Reconstruction that would leave the South and the former slaves in the control of exactly the same set of men who had led in four years of rebellion. Worse, Sherman could not restrain himself from voicing his approval in a letter to Johnson. Much to Sherman's consternation—and apparently genuine surprise—the politically beleaguered president seized on the support of the nation's second-greatest war hero and celebrity and in various ways tried to use Sherman to shore up his unpopular administration. Through the difficulties that followed, Sherman and Grant loyally helped each other to avoid political pitfalls. When he could, Grant shielded Sherman from assignments that seemed to be overtly political. Sherman, for his part, volunteered for a diplomatic mission to Mexico in place of Grant, whom Johnson had been trying to send for the purpose of getting him out of Washington and perhaps discrediting him.[6]

Grant and Sherman came through the difficult Johnson years politically unscathed and with their friendship as strong as ever. Better times seemed to be ahead when in 1868 Grant successfully ran for president. With Grant vacating the office of general-in-chief, Sherman was next in line, and in 1869, Sherman duly received it along with a promotion to lieutenant general. The new arrangement promised to solve a perennial problem in the administration of the army. For decades, secretaries of war and commanding generals had clashed incessantly because the secretary of war exercised direct control over all of the army's staff bureaus while the commanding general's authority was limited to actual operations. It was a silly distinction that could, with the wrong secretary of war, make a commanding general's task almost impossible. On his first day in office as president, Grant issued General Orders No. 11, placing the staff bureaus under the commanding general and requiring that all the secretary of war's orders to the army be issued through that general. Sherman was delighted.

Less than a month later, however, Grant rescinded the order. His secretary of war, John A. Rawlins, had accompanied him throughout the war as chief-of-staff, and the two were very close. Rawlins pressed Grant to restore the previous arrangement, and in an early indication that he would not be as good a president as he had been a general, Grant acquiesced. When Sherman remonstrated with him, Grant explained that Rawlins was in poor health, and Grant did not want to upset him. Sherman was deeply hurt, and the two men's relationship was never the same. "To me he is a mystery," Sherman said of Grant, "and I believe he is a mystery to himself."

Rawlins proved to be a reasonable secretary of war and usually forwarded his orders through Sherman, but Rawlins died of tuberculosis that fall, and in his place, Grant appointed W. W. Belknap of Iowa, a subordinate of Sherman's during the war. If Sherman thought Belknap would be reasonable, he was sadly mistaken, and with the Iowan's accession to office, the traditional feud between secretary and commanding general resumed with all its accustomed bitterness. Belknap effectively seized control of the army, and Sherman was left with little to do.[7]

Rather than engage in bureaucratic warfare with Belknap, Sherman preferred to busy himself elsewhere. In the spring of 1871, he made a lengthy inspection tour of army posts in the West. In Texas, he visited forts the army had built along the frontier to guard against the Comanche and Kiowa, traveling to San Antonio, for many years the army's headquarters in Texas. On May 2, he rode out of San Antonio accompanied by the army's inspector general, Randolph B. Marcy, who had sited some of these forts in the 1850s. They traveled northwest with two of Sherman's aides and a small escort, first to Fort Concho, near present-day San Angelo, and then over the next two weeks continued northeast to Forts Griffin, Belknap, and Richardson. Sherman was particularly interested in observing the conditions around Fort Richardson, the northernmost of the forts, because Texans had recently been complaining of frequent raids by Comanche and Kiowa from the Fort Sill Reservation in what is now Oklahoma. By May 17, when he reached Fort Richardson, Sherman had seen no Indians and was convinced that the Texans were exaggerating.

The following evening, however, a teamster stumbled into the fort on foot to report that his wagon train had been ambushed by a war party of over a hundred Kiowas and Comanches twenty miles west of the fort. That particular wagon train was headed by a civilian named Henry Warren, who had contracted with the army to haul supplies to the Texas forts. Sherman's party had met Warren's train on the way to Fort Richardson the day before, and, as Sherman would later learn, his party had ridden within half a mile of the war party, waiting concealed in ambush. Advised by their medicine man, and perhaps deterred by Sherman's escort of seventeen soldiers of the all-black Tenth U.S. Infantry, mounted for the occasion, they had allowed the high-ranking officers to pass undisturbed. Warren's wagon train had not fared so well. The Indians had attacked, killing Warren and six of his teamsters, mutilating some of the bodies, and capturing the supply shipment. Five teamsters had escaped, including the one who carried the news to Fort Richardson.

Sherman immediately ordered the post commander, Colonel Ranald S. Mackenzie, to mount an expedition in pursuit of the perpetrators, while Sherman and his party continued their journey to Fort Sill. There Sherman learned that Kiowa chief Satanta had arrived at the Fort Sill agency a few days before to collect his ration from the government and when questioned had boasted that with fellow chiefs Satank and Big Tree he had led the war party that had carried out the wagon train raid and the murders of Warren and his men. On May 27 Sherman confronted the chiefs on the front porch of the agent's house in a tense stand-off between armed Indians and Sherman's black soldiers. In the end, the Indians backed down, and Sherman arrested the three ringleaders of the raid. He had them shipped south to Jacksboro, Texas, near Fort Richardson, to be tried for murder under Texas law. Satank died in a suicidal escape attempt along the way. The other two were duly convicted and sentenced to hang, but the governor of Texas, pressured by humanitarian groups and fearing Kiowa reprisals, commuted their punishment to life imprisonment.

Convinced by the Warren wagon train raid that the Texans had not been overstating the Indian threat, Sherman ordered his commanders on the Texas frontier to take a more aggressive stance and attack any Indians found off the reservations. For two years, the presence of Satanta and Big Tree in the Texas penitentiary seemed to be a sufficient motivation for the Kiowa and Comanche to stay on their reservations. Then Eastern do-gooders and members of the federal Bureau of Indian Affairs prevailed on the Texas governor to parole the two chiefs, much to the disgust of Sherman, who suggested that when Satanta took his revenge, he hoped the governor's would be the first scalp taken. The chiefs returned to their tribe, and as Sherman had foreseen, the raids began again. Sherman urged his frontier commanders to move aggressively against the hostile Indians, and in the resulting Red River War they succeeded in driving the tribes back to the reservations and keeping them there.[8]

When Sherman returned to Washington, matters with Belknap were no better than they had been, so he took an opportunity of making a tour of Europe. His fame had made him a celebrity on the far side of the Atlantic as well, and he got to meet many of the crowned heads of Europe as well as other dignitaries. He would remember as "one of the most splendid sights I ever beheld" his experience of reviewing the Turkish fleet from the deck of the royal yacht of the sultan of Turkey, as it sailed up the Bosporus, receiving a twenty-one-gun salute. In Egypt, he climbed three-hundred feet up the side of the Great Pyramid of Cheops.[9]

He was gone the better part of a year, but of course when he returned he faced the same problem with the secretary of war, who effectively exercised the function of a general-in-chief, leaving the commanding general as a supernumerary. For 1873, Sherman declined to submit an annual report, pointing out that the secretary of war was actually commanding the army. The following year, he moved his headquarters from Washington, D.C., to St. Louis. It gave him even less control over the army, but it relieved him of the onerous necessity of dealing with politicians like Belknap.[10]

It was some satisfaction to Sherman, when early in 1876, Secretary Belknap was found to have been using his total control of the army to skim kickbacks from post traders, and thus, indirectly, from the long-suffering enlisted men. The case against him was so solid that Belknap hastily resigned while the House of Representatives was in the midst of considering his impeachment; nevertheless the House proceeded to impeach him anyway by unanimous vote, making him the only cabinet member ever to suffer impeachment. In Belknap's place, Grant appointed Ohio lawyer Alfonso Taft. Taft promised to consult Sherman before taking actions, and Sherman agreed to move his headquarters back to Washington. A few weeks later, Grant issued an order placing some of the staff bureaus under Sherman's command and specifying that henceforth the War Department's orders were to "be promulgated through the General of the Army." This change, coupled with the more reasonable behavior of Taft and subsequent secretaries of war, brought more harmonious relations and an end to the squabbles that had marked relations between secretaries and generals for decades—although the command system was not completely corrected until the early twentieth century.[11]

No general-in-chief could completely escape dealing with politicians, and over the years of his tenure Sherman had to cope with efforts by Congress to cut the size of the army—which he opposed—as well as to reform certain aspects of it—which he generally favored. In the end, troop strength remained at about the same inadequate level of roughly twenty-five thousand men, far less than was needed to police the Indian frontier. Sherman was a steadfast proponent of military professionalism and a strong supporter of the U.S. Military Academy at West Point. Sherman's support of West Point brought him into conflict with Senator John A. Logan, the man who had led the Army of the Tennessee to victory after McPherson's death at the July 22, 1864, Battle of Atlanta. Logan still begrudged what he saw as the West Point clique that had denied him the high command he believed he had earned. The two men finally reconciled after Sherman's retirement. In keeping with his commitment to military professionalism and education, Sherman in 1881 established the army's School of Application for Infantry and Cavalry at Fort Leavenworth, Kansas, a forerunner of the modern army's Command and General Staff College.[12]

By the early 1880s, Congress had passed an act that would require officers like Sherman to retire at the age of sixty-four but allowed him to retain full pay and benefits. He was concerned that by staying on longer, he would hold back lower-ranking officers like Philip H. Sheridan and John M. Schofield, and as always, he was tired of the squabbles with politicians—increasingly tired with every passing year. In October 1883, he forwarded a request through Secretary of War Robert Lincoln seeking the permission of President Chester A. Arthur to turn over command of the army to Sheridan on November 1 of that year and to relocate with his staff to St. Louis to await his sixty-fourth birthday the following February. Arthur agreed, and Sherman handed over command and left the capital. The president issued the formal order for his retirement right on time the following February, expressing the nation's "mingled emotions of regret and gratitude." Writing to thank Arthur, Sherman expressed his hope that when the president's order was read at regimental parades throughout the army "many a young hero will tighten his belt, and resolve anew to be brave and true to the starry flag, which we of our day have carried safely through one epoch of danger, but which may yet be subjected to other trials, which may demand similar sacrifices, equal fidelity and courage, and a larger measure of intelligence."[13]

That June, he traveled to West Point for the academy's graduation exercises. There he made a few brief remarks after General Alfred Terry's main commencement address. "In looking at this fine graduating class, even from this distance," he began, then paused, and finally continued, "you look exactly like the class last year, and the one before that, and the one of every year since the class that I graduated in." The crowd laughed. Sherman went on: "I can see myself and my old classmates, almost, in your features. I can see . . ."—and here he went on to name a dozen of his classmates. The reporter did not give the names, but perhaps one of them was George Thomas, who had died of a stroke in 1870. One whose name did make it into the newspaper report was Joe Blankster, a strapping six foot, five inch Ohioan, killed by a lightning strike while on duty in Florida many years before. Sherman urged the cadets to be honest and loyal to West Point. "If you don't love your profession, go away quick," he said, drawing to a close. "You may, one and all, become heroes, as others have before you." He promised to come back from time to time after that if he could and bade them all good-bye. The reporter noted that Sherman seemed to be deeply moved while giving his remarks, adding "Nearly every lady in the assemblage was in tears, and half the cadets were trying to conceal their faces." The band played "Auld Lang Syne," and the ceremony was over.[14]

As wistfully as he had approached his retirement, Sherman never looked back once it was done. Five years later, he boasted to a friend that he had not once meddled with the army since retiring. He took an interest in veterans' affairs but none at all in current military matters.[15]

He also took no interest in politics, asserting that for any man to enter that profession was like a virtuous maiden marrying a drunkard in hopes of reforming him. "It never has succeeded and never will." Even so, Sherman maintained, any would-be reformer of politics would find that "he will be carried along and involved in its scandals and unavoidable sins." He was therefore not even remotely tempted to accept when a strong draft-Sherman movement sprang up in anticipation of the 1884 election. He would rather, he quipped, spend a term in the penitentiary than in the presidency. Yet, despite his repeated demurrals politicians continued to bedevil him—partially because they could not conceive of any man who did not lust for high office and partially because they were accustomed to their fellow politicians coyly denying their own very real desire for the presidency. Everyone denied that he wanted the office, they thought, but everyone really did. Not Sherman—the politicians' importunities finally extracted from him his famously categorical "Shermanesque" refusal: "If drafted, I will not run; if nominated, I will not accept; if elected, I will not serve." That was something the politicians had to accept—until the next election cycle. Sherman had to fend off their blandishments every presidential election year for the rest of his life.[16]

Sherman at first retired to the fine house the people of St. Louis had given him, and there he and Ellen lived happily for two years. He had published the first edition of his memoirs in 1875, and in 1885, he brought out an updated edition. In 1886, the Shermans moved to New York to be closer to their grown children.[17]

Sherman and Ellen got along tolerably well. She still wished her husband would accept Catholicism, and he still wished she would spend less money. In 1878 their eldest son, Thomas, graduated from the law school of Washington University in St. Louis, as he previously had from Georgetown and Yale. Sherman had high hopes for him, believing that Thomas would insure the financial security of Ellen and the other children in case of his own early demise. He had secured for his son a promise of a position in the prominent St. Louis law firm of his old staff officer, Henry Hitchcock. Then, a few weeks after graduation, Thomas wrote to his father to say that he had decided to become a Jesuit priest. Sherman never forgave his son for what he regarded as the equivalent of desertion by a soldier. Meanwhile, in 1874, Minnie married a young naval officer who had subsequently left the service on Sherman's advice and entered the business world.[18]

In New York, the Shermans lived in the Fifth Street Hotel for two years, and then in September 1888, moved into a handsome brownstone at 75 West Seventy-first Street, near Central Park. In November of that year, Ellen died. She had been sickly for years, but Sherman had not considered her situation serious until the day before her death. It was a severe shock for him, and he became deeply depressed for a time. He gradually came out of it, but thereafter he seemed to feel his age much more as well as his own mortality. "I feel it coming sometimes when I get home from an entertainment or banquet," he told an old army comrade, "especially these winter nights. I feel death reaching out for me, as it were. I suppose I'll take cold some night and go to bed never to get up again."[19]

Still, he remained active. At a January 31 dinner of the New York Press Club in honor of African explorer Henry M. Stanley, Sherman formally responded to a toast to the "Old Army." "We realize that new boys are born as good as those in the past," he intoned. "They grow up into stout manhood and will take our places and be none the worse for the old traditions of courage, manhood, and fidelity passed down to them legitimately by the 'old army.'"[20]

One day the following week—much as he had predicted would happen—Sherman woke with a bad cold after an evening at the theater. The cold grew worse over the next few days and was joined by two chronic maladies that had plagued Sherman occasionally for years, asthma and a streptococcal inflammation of the face and neck. He passed his seventy-first birthday without festivities on February 8. The inflammation was severe enough that he could scarcely speak, and he spent the day reading Dickens. The following day his worsening condition prompted his physician to summon the family. Despite the onset of pneumonia, the old general fought on through the next week. He spoke little, but repeated several times the phrase he had asked to have placed on his tombstone: "Faithful and honorable." At 1:50 P.M., February 14, Sherman died surrounded by his family—daughters Minnie, Elly, and Lizzie, son Tecumseh, two sons-in-law, brother John, and brother-in-law Tom Ewing, Jr.[21]

Five days later, an impressive procession conducted Sherman's casket through the streets of New York to the tip of Manhattan. Thence, it traveled by ferry to Jersey City, and then by train to St. Louis to be interred next to Ellen, Willie, and Charles. Large crowds stood alongside the tracks to pay their respects as the train passed through cities, smaller groups, or individual families in the countryside. In St. Louis, son Thomas Sherman, now a priest, conducted the funeral service. Cannon boomed their salute; a detachment of the Thirteenth U.S. Infantry fired three volleys over the grave; and a bugler played taps.[22]

Sherman never doubted that the great achievement of his life had been his service in the Civil War. There, he had thoroughly earned his recognized status as the Union's second greatest general and secured for himself a claim to be counted by future generations as one of the nation's greatest generals. He was not without shortcomings as a general. He never possessed Grant's or Lee's ability to predict an opponent's actions. He lacked the killer instinct of Grant or Sheridan as well as Grant's ability—almost unique in his generation—to finish a victory by trapping and capturing the enemy army.

At offensive tactics, he was no better than average in an era when no officer had really solved the problem of overcoming enhanced defensive firepower.

Yet, his strengths far outweighed his weaknesses. He was profoundly cool in the heat of combat—much cooler amid the din of battle than in quiet contemplation of what an enemy general might be doing beyond the scope of his reconnaissance, and at Shiloh he showed himself a superb defensive commander—unremittingly tenacious and combative. In command of a major independent field force in 1864, Sherman came into his own and began to display his true genius. He may not have invented maneuver warfare—Grant had displayed a masterpiece of the art in his May 1863 Vicksburg Campaign—but Sherman certainly raised its practice to a new level. On a stage more than twice the size of the previous year's contest in Mississippi, Sherman maneuvered larger forces over longer distances against a much more formidable foe and vastly greater logistic challenges. With the exception of the attack at Kennesaw Mountain, he consistently avoided advancing into the enemy's strength and skillfully maneuvered into the enemy's areas of weakness. Adept at protecting his own supply lines, he proved equally adroit at threatening those of his opponent.

What he did on an operational level in the Atlanta Campaign, he practiced on a strategic level in the March to the Sea and the Carolinas Campaign. Having by that point in the war broken through the Confederacy's outer shell, he then penetrated deep into the enemy's hinterland destroying transportation, supplies, and manufacturing capacity, and sapping the morale both of the enemy civilians his troops encountered and of their soldier relatives then serving in the major Confederate armies. While he could have attacked and taken the Confederate manufacturing centers at Macon and Augusta, he chose instead to bypass them, capitalizing on the areas of weakness that his opponent had created in making Macon and Augusta relatively strong, and by destroying transportation, he ultimately rendered both places useless to his foes.

Sherman's mastery of maneuver warfare did not go unnoticed by history or by other military practitioners. In the 1920s, British army captain Basil H. Liddell Hart wrote a biography of Sherman, taking special note of Sherman's use of maneuver. Hart developed his own ideas on the subject, based both on his study of military history and on his experience in the First World War. Like Sherman, he advocated avoiding direct attacks on the enemy in position and taking instead the indirect approach. As Liddell Hart put it, "The longest way round is often the shortest way there." Sherman would have approved. Liddell Hart's work was in turn much admired and studied by German General Heinz Guderian. Taking Liddell Hart's ideas, along with those of others such as British theorist J. F. C. Fuller, Guderian further developed them into the Blitzkrieg. From studying the German Blitzkrieg, American General George H. Patton developed his own ideas of mobile warfare and successfully turned lightning war against its German progenitors. Thus, in a sense, Sherman's methods stand in direct linear succession to those of modern mobile warfare. The technology has changed and has continued to change, with more recent innovations such as air-land battle, but the concept of maneuvering against the enemy's weaknesses remains exactly what Sherman brought into full bloom in the closing year of the Civil War. Thus, one might say that Sherman's ideas are not only relevant to modern military operations, but that they are modern military operations—with refinements and adjustments for new technology.[23]

Finally, Sherman was a great general because of his personal qualities. He was a trusted and trustworthy subordinate. During the Civil War, both he and Grant were able to undertake operations they would not otherwise have tried because they knew they could trust each other implicitly. Sherman's loyalty and fidelity are qualities that are never outdated. They are as necessary in the modern world as they were during the nation's severest test. Their standard was one from which Sherman never deviated. As a soldier and a comrade he had remained, to the end, faithful and honorable.

Notes

Introduction

1. William Tecumseh Sherman, *Memoirs of General W. T. Sherman,* Michael Fellman, ed. (New York: Penguin, 2000), 514.
2. Brooks D. Simpson and Jean V. Berlin, *Sherman's Civil War,* 727, 729–30; Henry Hitchcock, *Marching with Sherman: Passages from the Letters and Campaign Diaries of Henry Hitchock,* M. A. DeWolfe Howe, ed. (Lincoln: University of Nebraska Press, 1995; originally published by Yale University Press, 1927), 21.

Chapter 1

1. William Tecumseh Sherman, *Memoirs of General W. T. Sherman,* Michael Fellman, ed. (New York: Penguin, 2000), 8–9; Carl R. Schenker, Jr., "'My Father . . . Named Me William Tecumseh': Rebutting the Charge that General Sherman Lied about His Name," *Ohio History,* vol. 115 (2008), pp. 55–79; Lee Kennett, *Sherman: A Soldier's Life* (New York: HarperCollins, 2001), 7; John F. Marszalek, *Sherman: A Soldier's Passion for Order* (New York: Free Press, 1993), 1–5.
2. Stanley P. Hirshson, *The White Tecumseh: A Biography of General William T. Sherman* (New York: John Wiley & Sons, 1997), 3; Kennett, *Sherman,* 8; Marszalek, *Sherman,* 1–5.
3. Sherman, *Memoirs,* 9–10; Hirshson, *The White Tecumseh,* 7; Kennett, *Sherman,* 8; Marszalek, *Sherman,* 5.
4. Marszalek, *Sherman,* 5–6.
5. Hirshson, *The White Tecumseh,* 5; Kennett, *Sherman,* 5.

6. Hirshson, *The White Tecumseh*, 5, 7; Kennett, *Sherman*, 9; Marszalek, *Sherman*, 9–10, 15.
7. Kennett, *Sherman*, 9–10; Marszalek, *Sherman*, 11–14.
8. Sherman, *Memoirs*, 11; Hirshson, *The White Tecumseh*, 8; Kennett, *Sherman*, 13–14.
9. Sherman, *Memoirs*, 12; Hirshson, *The White Tecumseh*, 8–11; Marszalek, *Sherman*, 16–23.
10. Hirshson, *The White Tecumseh*, 10–11; Kennett, *Sherman*, 17; Marszalek, *Sherman*, 20.
11. Sherman, *Memoirs*, 13; Hirshson, *The White Tecumseh*, 13–14; Marszalek, *Sherman*, 22–23.
12. Hirshson, *The White Tecumseh*, 11–13; Kennett, *Sherman*, 15, 19.
13. Kennett, *Sherman*, 23; Marszalek, *Sherman*, 25–27.
14. Hirshson, *The White Tecumseh*, 17; Kennett, *Sherman*, 15; Marszalek, *Sherman*, 22–31.
15. Sherman, *Memoirs*, 15, 18–20; Hirshson, *The White Tecumseh*, 18; Marszalek, *Sherman*, 33–38.
16. Sherman, *Memoirs*, 21; Hirshson, *The White Tecumseh*, 17–20; Kennett, *Sherman*, 26–27; Marszalek, *Sherman*, 33–39.
17. Sherman, *Memoirs*, 22–23; Kennett, *Sherman*, 28–31; Marszalek, *Sherman*, 39–42.
18. Sherman, *Memoirs*, 27–28; Hirshson, *The White Tecumseh*, 22–23; Kennett, *Sherman*, 31–32; Marszalek, *Sherman*, 41–46.
19. Sherman, *Memoirs*, 23–25; Kennett, *Sherman*, 32–34; Marszalek, *Sherman*, 46–48.
20. Hirshson, *The White Tecumseh*, 23, 25; Kennett, *Sherman*, 34–35; Marszalek, *Sherman*, 48–51.

Chapter 2

1. John S. D. Eisenhower, *So Far from God: The U.S. War with Mexico, 1846–1848* (New York: Random House, 1989), 17–20.
2. Eisenhower, *So Far from God*, 45–65.
3. Sherman, *Memoirs*, 29–30; Hirshson, *The White Tecumseh*, 26; Kennett, *Sherman*, 37–38; Marszalek, *Sherman*, 52–53.
4. Sherman, *Memoirs*, 30–31; Hirshson, *The White Tecumseh*, 26; Kennett, *Sherman*, 38; Marszalek, *Sherman*, 54–55.
5. Sherman, *Memoirs*, 31–35; Hirshson, *The White Tecumseh*, 27; Kennett, *Sherman*, 39; Marszalek, *Sherman*, 55–61.
6. Hirshson, *The White Tecumseh*, 29; Kennett, *Sherman*, 40–42; Marszalek, *Sherman*, 64–68.
7. Sherman, *Memoirs*, 54–55; Marszalek, *Sherman*, 68–69.

8. Sherman, *Memoirs,* 60–61; Hirshson, *The White Tecumseh,* 30–31; Marszalek, *Sherman,* 69–70.

9. Sherman, *Memoirs,* 65–66; Kennett, *Sherman,* 45–46; Marszalek, *Sherman,* 70.

10. Sherman, *Memoirs,* 75; Hirshson, *The White Tecumseh,* 30–31; Kennett, *Sherman,* 47; Marszalek, *Sherman,* 72–73.

11. Sherman, *Memoirs,* 86–87; Kennett, *Sherman,* 47–49; Marszalek, *Sherman,* 73–75.

12. Sherman, *Memoirs,* 86–87; Hirshson, *The White Tecumseh,* 32; Kennett, *Sherman,* 51; Marszalek, *Sherman,* 76–77.

13. Sherman, *Memoirs,* 87–89; Hirshson, *The White Tecumseh,* 33; Kennett, *Sherman,* 51–52; Marszalek, *Sherman,* 77–82.

14. Sherman, *Memoirs,* 90–91; Hirshson, *The White Tecumseh,* 33–34; Kennett, *Sherman,* 53; Marszalek, *Sherman,* 83–84.

15. Sherman, *Memoirs,* 92; Hirshson, *The White Tecumseh,* 34–35; Kennett, *Sherman,* 54–55; Marszalek, *Sherman,* 84–87.

16. Kennett, *Sherman,* 56–57; Marszalek, *Sherman,* 87–89.

17. Sherman, *Memoirs,* 94–95; Hirshson, *The White Tecumseh,* 36–37; Kennett, *Sherman,* 57–60; Marszalek, *Sherman,* 90–91.

18. Sherman, *Memoirs,* 95–96; Hirshson, *The White Tecumseh,* 38; Kennett, *Sherman,* 60–61; Marszalek, *Sherman,* 91–92.

19. Sherman, *Memoirs,* 96–103; Hirshson, *The White Tecumseh,* 39–40; Kennett, *Sherman,* 63–64; Marszalek, *Sherman,* 92–95.

20. Hirshson, *The White Tecumseh,* 40; Kennett, *Sherman,* 72–73; Marszalek, *Sherman,* 95–98.

21. Sherman, *Memoirs,* 109–14; Hirshson, *The White Tecumseh,* 44; Kennett, *Sherman,* 6–67; Marszalek, *Sherman,* 99–101.

22. Sherman, *Memoirs,* 116–22; Hirshson, *The White Tecumseh,* 47–49; Kennett, *Sherman,* 69–71; Marszalek, *Sherman,* 103–08.

23. Sherman, *Memoirs,* 128; Hirshson, *The White Tecumseh,* 50–51; Kennett, *Sherman,* 79–80; Marszalek, *Sherman,* 110–12.

24. Kennett, *Sherman,* 81; Marszalek, *Sherman,* 112–13.

25. Sherman, *Memoirs,* 129–31; Hirshson, *The White Tecumseh,* 52–54; Kennett, *Sherman,* 80–81; Marszalek, *Sherman,* 113.

26. Hirshson, *The White Tecumseh,* 54; Kennett, *Sherman,* 80–82; Marszalek, *Sherman,* 113–14.

27. Sherman, *Memoirs,* 133; Hirshson, *The White Tecumseh,* 46, 55–57; Kennett, *Sherman,* 82; Marszalek, *Sherman,* 115.

28. Sherman, *Memoirs,* 133–35; Hirshson, *The White Tecumseh,* 58–62; Kennett, *Sherman,* 83; Marszalek, *Sherman,* 115–19.

29. Sherman, *Memoirs,* 136–39; Hirshson, *The White Tecumseh,* 63–67; Kennett, *Sherman,* 85–88; Marszalek, *Sherman,* 120–26.

30. Sherman, *Memoirs,* 138–43; Hirshson, *The White Tecumseh,* 67–71; Kennett, *Sherman,* 87–88; Marszalek, *Sherman,* 126–27.

31. Sherman, *Memoirs,* 143; Marszalek, *Sherman,* 133–35.

32. Sherman, *Memoirs,* 143–52; Hirshson, *The White Tecumseh,* 74–78; Kennett, *Sherman,* 93; Marszalek, *Sherman,* 135–39.

Chapter 3

1. Sherman, *Memoirs,* 155; Marszalek, *Sherman,* 140–41.

2. Sherman, *Memoirs,* 156–57; Marszalek, *Sherman,* 141.

3. Sherman, *Memoirs,* 157; Marszalek, *Sherman,* 141–43.

4. Sherman, *Memoirs,* 160; Marszalek, *Sherman,* 143–44.

5. Sherman, *Memoirs,* 160–62; Marszalek, *Sherman,* 145–46.

6. Sherman, *Memoirs,* 162–66; Marszalek, *Sherman,* 146–47.

7. Marszalek, *Sherman,* 147–48.

8. Sherman, *Memoirs,* 167; Marszalek, *Sherman,* 149–50; Ethan S. Rafuse, *A Single Grand Victory: The First Campaign and Battle of Manassas* (Wilmington, DE: SR Books, 2002), 85; On the Union's conciliatory policy, see Mark Grimsley, *The Hard Hand of War: Union Military Policy toward Southern Civilians, 1861–1865* (New York: Cambridge University Press, 1995). 23–95.

9. Sherman, *Memoirs,* 167–68, 173; Rafuse, *A Single Grand Victory,* 102–10.

10. Marszalek, *Sherman,* 150; Rafuse, *A Single Grand Victory,* 117.

11. Sherman, *Memoirs,* 173; William C. Davis, *Battle at Bull Run: A History of the First Major Campaign of the Civil War* (Garden City, NY: Doubleday, 1977), 159; Rafuse, *A Single Grand Victory,* 120.

12. Sherman, *Memoirs,* 173; Davis, *Battle at Bull Run,* 160–64; Rafuse, *A Single Grand Victory,* 120.

13. Sherman, *Memoirs,* 173; Davis, *Battle at Bull Run,* 164, 185; Rafuse, *A Single Grand Victory,* 134–36.

14. Sherman, *Memoirs,* 173; Davis, *Battle at Bull Run,* 185–87; Rafuse, *A Single Grand Victory,* 137–39.

15. Davis, *Battle at Bull Run,* 217.

16. Sherman, *Memoirs,* 173; Davis, *Battle at Bull Run,* 217–18; Rafuse, *A Single Grand Victory,* 175–82.

17. Marszalek, *Sherman,* 150–51.

18. Sherman, *Memoirs,* 174.

19. Marszalek, *Sherman,* 151.

20. Sherman, *Memoirs,* 174–75; Marszalek, *Sherman,* 151–52.

21. Sherman, *Memoirs,* 175–76; Marszalek, *Sherman,* 152.

22. Sherman, *Memoirs,* 176.

23. Sherman, *Memoirs,* 177–78; Kennett, *Sherman,* 127–28.

24. Sherman, *Memoirs*, 179–83.
25. Sherman, *Memoirs*, 183; Hirshson, *The White Tecumseh*, 97–98.
26. Sherman, *Memoirs*, 183–84.
27. Marszalek, *Sherman*, 160; Kennett, *Sherman*, 135–36.
28. Sherman, *Memoirs*, 184–87, 193–97.
29. Sherman, *Memoirs*, 187, 189; Marszalek, *Sherman*, 162–63.
30. Marszalek, *Sherman*, 162–63.
31. Sherman, *Memoirs*, 198; Marszalek, *Sherman*, 164.
32. Sherman, *Memoirs*, 198; Marszalek, *Sherman*, 164.
33. Marszalek, *Sherman*, 164–66; Kennett, *Sherman*, 138–40.
34. Sherman, *Memoirs*, 201–3.
35. Sherman, *Memoirs*, 203–4.

Chapter 4

1. Ulysses S. Grant, *Personal Memoirs of U. S. Grant* 2, vols. (New York: Charles L. Webster, 1885), 1:315; Brooks D. Simpson and Jean V. Berlin, eds. *Sherman's Civil War: Selected Correspondence of William T. Sherman, 1860–1865* (Chapel Hill: University of North Carolina Press, 1999), 192–93; Sherman, *Memoirs*, 208; E. C. Dawes, "My First Day Under Fire at Shiloh," *Papers of the Military Order of the Loyal Legion of the United States*, 56 vols., (various publishers and dates; reprint, Wilmington, NC: Broadfoot Publishing Co., 1994. Hereinafter cited as MOLLUS), 3:2; U.S. War Department, *The War of the Rebellion: Official Records of the Union and Confederate Armies*, 128 vols. (Washington, D.C.: Government Printing Office, 1881–1901. Hereinafter cited as OR. Except as otherwise noted, all references are to series 1), vol. 10, pt. 1, 28; pt. 2, 11–12, 20; Simpson and Berlin, eds., *Sherman's Civil War*, 195; Lucien B. Crooker, Henry S. Nourse, and John G. Brown, *The 55th Illinois, 1861–1865* (Huntington, WV: Blue Acorn Press, 1993), 63.
2. Sherman, *Memoirs*, 209; OR vol. 10, pt. 1,. 8, 22.
3. Simpson and Berlin, eds., *Sherman's Civil War*, 197; Sherman, *Memoirs*, 209–10; OR vol. 10, pt 1, 22–23; Crooker, Nourse, and Brown, *The 55th Illinois*, 64; Robert H. Flemming, "The Battle of Shiloh as a Private Saw It," MOLLUS 6:132–33; Christian Zook to "Dear friends," March 23, 1862, Robert H. Christian Zook Papers, Civil War Miscellaneous Collection, U.S. Army Military History Institute, Carlisle, PA.
4. Sherman, *Memoirs*, 210; OR vol. 10, pt. 1, 23.
5. Sherman, *Memoirs*, 210–11; OR vol. 10, pt. 1, 84; pt. 2, 53–54, 67.

6. Sherman, *Memoirs,* 211; OR vol. 10, pt. 2, 15, 21, 32, 70; Brooks D. Simpson, *Ulysses S. Grant: Triumph over Adversity, 1822–1865* (New York: Houghton Mifflin, 2000), 123–27; Jean Edward Smith, *Grant* (New York: Simon & Schuster, 2001), 176–79.

7. OR vol. 10, pt. 2, 46, 50–51.

8. Sherman, *Memoirs,* 211–12; OR vol. 10, pt. 1, 90; Thomas W. Connelly, *History of the Seventieth Ohio Regiment* (Cincinnati: Peak Bros., n.d.), 19–20.

9. Sherman, *Memoirs,* 211–12; OR vol. 10, pt. 1, 93.

10. Flemming, "The Battle of Shiloh as a Private Saw It," MOLLUS 6:136–38.

11. Edward Gordon, "A Graphic Picture of the Battle of Shiloh," *National Tribune,* April 26, 1888, 1; OR vol. 10, pt. 2,. 93–94.

12. E. C. Dawes, "My First Day Under Fire at Shiloh," MOLLUS 3:3–5.

13. Dawes, "My First Day Under Fire at Shiloh," MOLLUS, 3:3–5; Gordon, "A Graphic Picture of the Battle of Shiloh," *National Tribune,* May 3, 1883, 3; Charles F. Hubert, *History of the Fiftieth Regiment, Illinois Volunteer Infantry in the War of the Union* (Kansas City, MO: Western Veteran Publishing Co., 1894), 89.

14. Sherman, *Memoirs,* 212.

15. Dawes, "My First Day Under Fire at Shiloh," MOLLUS 3:5–7.

16. Gordon, "A Graphic Picture of the Battle of Shiloh," *National Tribune,* May 3, 1883, 3; Dawes, "My First Day Under Fire at Shiloh," MOLLUS 3:7–8

17. Gordon, "A Graphic Picture of the Battle of Shiloh," *National Tribune,* May 3, 1883, 1, 3; John A. Cockerill, "A Boy at Shiloh," MOLLUS 6:17.

18. Connelly, *History of the Seventieth Ohio Regiment,* 22.

19. Douglas Putnam, "Reminiscences of the Battle of Shiloh," MOLLUS 2:198–207; OR vol. 10, pt. 1, 180, 185; Smith, *Grant,* 191–92; Grant, *Personal Memoirs,* 1:343.

20. Larry J. Daniel, *Shiloh: The Battle that Changed the Civil War* (New York: Simon & Schuster, 1997), 182–85.

21. Simpson, *Ulysses S. Grant,* 134.

22. Sherman, *Memoirs,* 225–27.

23. John Y. Simon, ed., *The Papers of Ulysses S. Grant,* 26 vols. (Carbondale: Southern Illinois University Press, 1969), 5:34.

24. Simpson, *Ulysses S. Grant,* 137; Marion Morrison, *A History of the Ninth Regiment Illinois Volunteer Infantry* (Monmouth, IL, 1864; reprint, Carbondale: Southern Illinois University Press, 1997), 34.

25. Sherman, *Memoirs,* 228–29.

26. Brooks D. Simpson, "After Shiloh: Grant, Sherman, and Survival," in Steven E. Woodworth, ed., *The Shiloh Campaign* (Carbondale: Southern Illinois University Press, 2009).

27. Simpson, "After Shiloh"; Sherman, *Memoirs,* 231–36; OR vol. 10, pt. 2, 105–06; Simon, ed., *Papers of Ulysses S. Grant,* 5:48–52; Grant, *Personal Memoirs,* 1:379.

28. Sherman, *Memoirs,* 238–58; OR vol. 13, 748–49; vol. 17, pt. 2, 280–82, 285, 856–57; Simpson and Berlin, eds., *Sherman's Civil War,* 346–47.

29. Sherman, *Memoirs,* 259–60; Simon, ed., *Papers of Ulysses S. Grant,* 6:243, 256, 262, 293, 310–12; OR vol. 17, pt. 1,. 466–67, 471.

30. Jenney, "Personal Recollections of Vicksburg," MOLLUS 12:248–49.

31. James W. Denver to "My Dear Wife," November 29, 1862, James W. Denver Papers, Harrisburg Civil War Round Table Collection, U.S. Army Military History Institute, Carlisle, PA.

32. Sherman, *Memoirs,* 260–62; Simon, ed., *Papers of Ulysses S. Grant,* 6:372, 403; OR vol. 17, pt, 1, 473–74; Grant, *Personal Memoirs,* 1:428–32.

33. Sherman, *Memoirs,* 264–69; Simpson and Berlin, eds., *Sherman's Civil War,* 342–43; Crooker, Nourse, and Brown, *The 55th Illinois,* 186.

34. Sherman, *Memoirs,* 269–70; OR vol. 17, pt. 1, 651–52.

35. Sherman, *Memoirs,* 270–71; OR vol. 17, pt. 1, 625, 647, 650, 655–56.

36. Sherman, *Memoirs,* 271–72; Sherman to Porter, December 29, 1862; Sherman Papers, Huntington Library.

37. Sherman, *Memoirs,* 272–76.

38. Sherman, *Memoirs,* 276–82; Grant, *Personal Memoirs,* 1:441.

Chapter 5

1. OR vol. 24, pt. 1, 8, 10; Jenney, "Personal Recollections of Vicksburg," MOLLUS 12:252; Crooker, Nourse, and Brown, *The 55th Illinois,* 211.

2. William L. B. Jenney, "With Sherman and Grant from Memphis to Chattanooga: A Reminiscence," MOLLUS 13:198–99; Sherman, *Memoirs,* 282.

3. OR vol. 24, pt. 1, 20–21; Sherman, *Memoirs,* 283–84.

4. Grant, *Personal Memoirs,* 1:452–53; Sherman, *Memoirs,* 284.

5. Sherman, *Memoirs,* 284–85.

6. Sherman, *Memoirs,* 285–86; OR vol. 24, pt. 1, 440–41, 443–44.

7. Sherman, *Memoirs,* 290–92.

8. Sherman, *Memoirs,* 294.
9. Sherman, *Memoirs,* 294–95; Simon, ed., *The Papers of Ulysses S. Grant,* 8:130–31; OR vol. 24, pt. 1, 576–77.
10. Sherman, *Memoirs,* 296.
11. Sherman, *Memoirs,* 297; Grant, *Personal Memoirs,* 1:505; OR vol. 24, pt. 1, 50–51.
12. Sherman, *Memoirs,* 297; Grant, *Personal Memoirs,* 1:506–07; OR vol. 24, pt. 1,–51.
13. Sherman, *Memoirs,* 297; Grant, *Personal Memoirs,* 1:507.
14. Sherman, *Memoirs,* 297; Grant, *Personal Memoirs,* 1:507, 511–12.
15. Sherman, *Memoirs,* 297.
16. Sherman, *Memoirs,* 298–99; OR vol. 24, pt. 1, 53–54.
17. Sherman, *Memoirs,* 299–300; OR vol. 24, pt. 1, 54.
18. Sherman, *Memoirs,* 300; OR vol. 24, pt. 2, 257; 264, 268.
19. Sherman, *Memoirs,* 300–01; Grant, *Personal Memoirs,* 1:531.
20. Sherman, *Memoirs,* 301; Grant, *Personal Memoirs,* 1:531.
21. Sherman, *Memoirs,* 301; Grant, *Personal Memoirs,* 1:531; OR vol. 24, pt. 1, 55–56, 172; pt. 2, 232, 240; Jenney "Personal Recollections of Vicksburg," MOLLUS 12:261.
22. Sherman, *Memoirs,* 301; Grant, *Personal Memoirs,* 1:531; OR vol. 24, pt. 1, 55–56; Jenney "Personal Recollections of Vicksburg," MOLLUS 12:261.
23. Edwin Cole Bearss, *The Campaign for Vicksburg.* (3. vols.) Vol. 3, *Unvexed to the Sea.* (Dayton, OH: Morningside House, 1986), 847–52; OR vol. 24, pt. 1, p. 733.
24. Byron Cloyd Bryner, *Bugle Echoes: The Story of the Illinois 47th* (Springfield, IL: Philip Bros., Printers, 1905) 85–86; J. W. Greenman Diary, May 23, 1862, Mississippi Department of Archives and History; Burdette, Robert J. *Drums of the 47th* (Indianapolis: Bobbs-Merrill, 1914). 68–69.
25. Jenney, "Personal Recollections of Vicksburg," MOLLUS 12:261; Sanborn, "The Campaign against Vicksburg," MOLLUS 27:134.
26. OR vol. 24, pt. 1, 88, 90–91.
27. John B. Sanborn, "Remarks on a Motion to Extend a Vote of Thanks to General Marshall for above Paper," MOLLUS 29:612; W. R. Eddington Reminiscences, Civil War Miscellaneous Papers, U.S. Army Military History Institute, Carlisle, PA.
28. OR vol. 24, pt. 1, 161–63; Jenney, "Personal Recollections of Vicksburg," MOLLUS 12:262.
29. OR vol. 24, pt. 1, 162–64.
30. OR vol. 24, pt. 1, 159–86; Bearss, *Unvexed to the Sea,* 879–80; Jenney, "Personal Recollections of Vicksburg," MOLLUS 12:262–63.
31. OR vol. 24, pt. 1, 105.

32. Sherman, *Memoirs,* 303–04.
33. OR vol. 24, pt. 1, 57–56.
34. Sherman, *Memoirs,* 305–06.

Chapter 6

1. Sherman, *Memoirs,* 308.
2. Sherman, *Memoirs,* 308–15.
3. Sherman, *Memoirs,* 315.
4. Sherman, *Memoirs,* 317–18.
5. Sherman, *Memoirs,* 319–20.
6. Sherman, *Memoirs,* 320.
7. Sherman, *Memoirs,* 320–21.
8. Sherman, *Memoirs,* 324–35.
9. Sherman, *Memoirs,* 329; Grant, *Personal Memoirs,* 2:45; Wiley Sword, *Mountains Touched with Fire: Chattanooga Besieged, 1863* (New York: St. Martin's, 1995), 51; Horace Porter, *Campaigning with Grant* (New York: Bonanza Books, 1961), 5–6.
10. Sherman, *Memoirs,* 331–32; Jabez Banbury Diary, November 4–6 and 10, 1863, "Enoch Wiess Reminiscences," and "W. G. McElrea Diary, November 13, 1863," all in *The Civil War Miscellaneous Collection,* U.S. Army Military History Institute, Carlisle, Pennsylvania; Crooker, Nourse, and Brown, *The 55th Illinois,* 277–78; John Quincy Adams Campbell, *The Union Must Stand: The Civil War Diary of John Quincy Adams Campbell, Fifth Iowa Volunteer Infantry,* Mark Grimsley and Todd D. Miller, eds. (Knoxville: University of Tennesee Press, 2000), 134–36; Connelly, *History of the Seventieth Ohio Regiment,* 56.
11. John F. Marszalek, "'Take the Seat of Honor': William T. Sherman," in *Grant's Lieutenants: From Chattanooga to Appomattox,* Steven E. Woodworth, ed., (Lawrence: University Press of Kansas), 2008.
12. Sherman, *Memoirs,* 343; Marszalek, "'Take the Seat of Honor,'" 7.
13. Sherman, *Memoirs,* 333–34.
14. Crooker, Nourse, and Brown, *The 55th Illinois,* 281–84; OR vol. 31, pt. 2, 572–73; Jabez Banbury Diary; Campbell, *The Union Must Stand,* 134–36.
15. OR vol. 31, pt. 2, 573, 629, 646; Campbell, *The Union Must Stand,* 34–36; 224–27; Connelly, *History of the Seventieth Ohio Regiment,* 60–61; Taylor, *Tom Taylor's Civil War,* 84–87; Crooker, Nourse, and Brown, *The 55th Illinois,* 282–84.
16. OR vol. 31, pt. 2,. 43–44.
17. Marszalek, "'Take the Seat of Honor,'" 8.
18. Sherman, *Memoirs,* 350–56; Marszalek, "'Take the Seat of Honor,'" 10.

19. Grant, *Personal Memoirs,* 2:107.

20. Marszalek, "'Take the Seat of Honor,'" 10.

21. Sherman, *Memoirs,* 360–63; OR vol. 32, pt. 1, 174; David W. Poak to "Dear Sister," February 1, 1864, David W. Poak Papers, Illinois State Historical Library; William W. McCarty Diary, February 2, 1864, *Civil War Miscellaneous Collection,* U.S. Army Military History Institute, Carlisle, PA.

22. Sherman, *Memoirs,* 361; Jessee, *Civil War Diaries,* chap. 5,. 6; Hosea W. Rood, *Story of the Service of Company E, Twelfth Wisconsin Regiment Veteran Volunteer Infantry in the War of the Rebellion* (Milwaukee: Swain & Tate, 1893), 242. OR vol. 32, pt. 1–175; pt. 2, 67.

23. Barber, *Army Memoirs,* 135; Jessee, *Civil War Diaries,* chap. 5, 8.

24. Sherman, *Memoirs,* 361; Rood, *Story of the Service of Company E,* 244–45; Jessee, *Civil War Diaries,* chap. 5, 7; William W. McCarty Diary, February 6. 1864, Civil War Miscellaneous Collection, U.S. Army Military History Institute, Carlisle, PA.

25. Sherman, *Memoirs,* 361–62.

26. Sherman, *Memoirs,* 362; OR vol. 32, pt. 1. 175

Chapter 7

1. Simpson and Berlin, eds., *Sherman's Civil War,* 618.

2. Sherman, *Memoirs,* 383–84.

3. Simpson and Berlin, eds., *Sherman's Civil War,* 617–18.

4. Simpson and Berlin, eds., *Sherman's Civil War,* 618.

5. Gary D. Joiner, *One Damned Blunder from Beginning to End: The Red River Campaign of 1864* (Wilmington, DE: Scholarly Resources, 2003).

6. John J. McKee Diary, May 4 and 8, 1864, Civil War Miscellaneous Collection, U.S. Army Military History Institute; OR vol. 38, pt. 3, 16, 169, 375; McMurry, *Atlanta 1864,* 50–58.

7. OR vol. 38, pt. 3, 16–17, 376, 398, 457, 483; pt. 4, 126–28, 138–40, 152–53, 691–97.

8. Castel, *Decision in the West,* 150.

9. OR vol. 38, pt. 124, 126–27, 141–43, 176–77, 190–91, 213, 220, 225, 376–78, 392–94, 399–401, 422, 439, 447–48, 457, 461; pt. 4, 200–1.

10. Sherman, *Memoirs,* 412–18; OR vol. 38, pt. 3, 33, 186, 205–6.

11. Sherman, *Memoirs,* 418; OR vol. 38, pt. 4, 260.

12. Sherman, *Memoirs,* 418; OR vol. 38, pt. 3, 16, 375–76, 397, 452, 457.

13. Sherman, *Memoirs,* 418–19; OR vol. 38, pt. 4, 288–89, 292–93.

14. Sherman, *Memoirs,* 419–21; OR vol. 38, pt. 3, 97; pt. 4, 404, 407.

15. Sherman, *Memoirs,* 427–28.
16. OR vol. 38, pt. 4, 480.
17. OR vol. 38, pt. 3, pp. 97–98, 279, 317, 337; pt. 4, 488–89.
18. OR vol. 38, pt, 4, 372–73.
19. OR vol. 38, pt. 3, 98–99, 179–80; pt. 4, 595, 601, 605–6.
20. Sherman, *Memoirs,* 434.
21. Sherman, *Memoirs,* 435.
22. Sherman, *Memoirs,* 438.
23. Sherman, *Memoirs,* 439–42; OR vol. 38, pt. 5, p. 65–66.

Chapter 8

1. OR vol. 38, pt. 5,. 65–66.
2. Sherman, *Memoirs,* 444; OR vol. 38, pt. 5, 149–50, 158, 220.
3. OR vol. 38, pt. 5, 170.
4. Sherman, *Memoirs,* 444; OR vol. 38, pt. 5, 188.
5. Nutt E. E., "Fight at Atlanta: Work of the Seventy-eighth and Twentieth Ohio That Day," *National Tribune,* January 3, 1884,. 3; William E. Strong, "The Death of General James B. McPherson," in MOLLUS 10:320–22, 324; John W. Fuller, "A Terrible Day," *National Tribune,* April 16, 1885,. 1; OR vol. 38, pt. 3,. 369–70, 418, 475, 545; Richard Tuthill, "An Artilleryman's Recollections of the Battle of Atlanta," MOLLUS 10:298–99; Gilbert D. Munson, "Battle of Atlanta," MOLLUS 2:219–20.
6. OR vol. 38, pt. 3, 20, 370, 450–51, 476, 543–44, 580, 746, 952; Leggett, "Battle of Atlanta," 5–6, 10–11.
7. OR vol. 38, pt. 3, 476; Leggett, "Battle of Atlanta," 6–7, 9; Leggett, "Battle of Atlanta," *National Tribune,* May 6, 1886, 1.
8. Leggett, "Battle of Atlanta," *National Tribune,* May 6, 1886, 25; Strong, "The Death of General James B. McPherson," MOLLUS 10:334–35.
9. OR vol. 38, pt. 3, 102, 139, 179, 231, 417, 425, 544–45, 581; Strong, "The Death of General James B. McPherson," MOLLUS 10:317; Leggett, "Battle of Atlanta." 1.
10. OR vol. 38, pt. 3, 102; pt. 5, 231; Strong, "The Death of General James B. McPherson," MOLLUS 10:317–19.
11. Strong, "The Death of General James B. McPherson," MOLLUS 10:319; Sherman, *Memoirs,* 449.
12. Sherman, *Memoirs,* 448–49.
13. Sherman, *Memoirs,* 449; Simpson and Berlin, eds., *Sherman's Civil War,* 682; OR vol. 38, pt. 1, 73.
14. Sherman, *Memoirs,* 449; OR vol. 38, pt. 5,. 233.
15. Sherman, *Memoirs,* 449; OR vol. 38, pt. 173; pt. 5, p. 241.

16. Steven E. Woodworth, *Nothing but Victory: The Army of the Tennessee, 1861–1865* (New York: Knopf, 2005), 553–68.
17. Sherman, *Memoirs,* 449–53; OR vol. 38, pt. 5, 235.
18. Gilbert D. Munson, "Battle of Atlanta," MOLLUS 2:229; Elisha Stockwell, Jr., *Private Elisha Stockwell, Jr., sees the Civil War.* Byron R. Abernathy, ed. (Norman: University of Oklahoma Press, 1958), 97–98; Taylor, Tom *Taylor's Civil War,* 151; Charles B. Loop to "My Dear Wife," July 26, 1864, Charles B. Loop Papers, Civil War Miscellaneous Collection, U.S. Army Military History Institute, Carlisle, PA.
19. Rood, *Story of the Service of Company E,* 319; William S. Covill to "Dear Sister," August 4, 1864; Jonathan Blair Papers, Illinois State Historical Library, Springfield.
20. Sherman, *Memoirs,* 456–57.
21. W. T. Sherman to John A. Logan, July 27, 1864, John A. Logan Papers, Library of Congress.
22. Sherman, *Memoirs,* 457; OR vol. 38, pt. 5, 272–73.
23. OR vol. 38, pt. 5, 255–56.
24. Howard, "The Struggle for Atlanta," 319; Oliver O. Howard, *Autobiography of Oliver Otis Howard, Major General, United States Army,* 2 vols. (Freeport, NY: Books for Libraries Press, 1971), 2:19–21.
25. OR vol. 38, pt. 3, 140; pt. 5,. 282; Connelly, *History of the Seventieth Ohio Regiment,* 97–98; Howard, "The Struggle for Atlanta," 319.
26. Sherman, *Memoirs,* 461.
27. Sherman, *Memoirs,* 462.
28. OR vol. 38, pt. 5, 408–09.
29. OR vol. 38, pt. 5, 763, 767–69, 777.
30. OR vol. 38, pt. 5, 794.

Chapter 9

1. Sherman, *Memoirs,* 479–81, 485–86; OR vol. 39, pt. 2, 364, 412–13.
2. Simpson and Berlin, eds. *Sherman's Civil War,* 713, 715.
3. Sherman, *Memoirs,* 479; OR vol. 38, pt. 5, 794, 822; vol. 39, pt. 2, 414.
4. Sherman, *Memoirs,* 489–92; OR vol. 39, pt. 2, pp. 416, 419–22.
5. Sherman, *Memoirs,* 492–95; OR vol. 39, pt. 2, 417–19.
6. Sherman, *Memoirs,* 505–10; OR vol. 39, pt. 2, 381, 395–96.
7. Sherman, *Memoirs,* 508–09, 532; OR vol. 39, pt. 2, pp. 464, 478.
8. Sherman, *Memoirs,* 508–10, 532–33; OR vol. 39, pt. 1, 3435.
9. Sherman, *Memoirs,* 513–14.

10. Sherman, *Memoirs,* 514–15, 518; OR vol. 39, pt. 1,. 731.

11. Sherman, *Memoirs,* 512, 519, 533; OR vol. 34, pt. 135; vol. 39, pt. 2, 79.

12. OR vol. 34, pt. 1, 35; vol. 39, pt. 2162.

13. Sherman, *Memoirs,* 519–20; OR vol. 34, pt. 1, 35–36.

14. Sherman, *Memoirs,* 523; OR vol. 39, pt. 2, 239–40.

15. Sherman, *Memoirs,* 529; OR vol. 39, pt. 2, 324–25; Henry Hitchcock, *Marching with Sherman: Passages from the Letters and Campaign Diaries of Henry Hitchock,* M. A. DeWolfe Howe, ed. (Lincoln: University of Nebraska Press, 1995; originally published by Yale University Press, 1927), 21.

16. Sherman, *Memoirs,* 530; OR vol. 39, pt. 2, 576.

17. Sherman, *Memoirs,* 530–31; OR vol. 39, pt. 2, 594–95.

18. Sherman, *Memoirs,* 531–32; OR vol. 39, pt. 2, 594.

19. Sherman, *Memoirs,* 534; OR vol. 39, pt. 2, 679.

20. Sherman, *Memoirs,* 534–35.

21. Hitchcock, *Marching with Sherman,* 58; OR vol. 44, 8.

22. Sherman, *Memoirs,* 542–43; Hitchcock, *Marching with Sherman,* 57; OR vol. 39, pt. 2, 578.

23. Sherman, *Memoirs,* 544; Hitchcock, *Marching with Sherman,* 59–61; OR vol. 44,. 8.

24. Sherman, *Memoirs,* 540–41; OR vol. 39, pt. 2, 713–14.

25. Sherman, *Memoirs,* 547; Hitchcock, *Marching with Sherman,* 75, 88.

26. Hitchcock, *Marching with Sherman,* 67, 83.

27. Hitchcock, *Marching with Sherman,* 77.

28. Sherman, *Memoirs,* 549; Hitchcock, *Marching with Sherman,* 84–85.

29. Sherman, *Memoirs,* 545–46, 549–50; Hitchcock, *Marching with Sherman,* 65–67, 70–71, 82, 84.

30. Sherman, *Memoirs,* 550–51; Hitchcock, *Marching with Sherman,* 89.

31. Sherman, *Memoirs,* 555–56; Hitchcock, *Marching with Sherman,* 133–35.

32. Sherman, *Memoirs,* 556–57; Hitchcock, *Marching with Sherman,* 161–62; OR vol. 44, 791.

33. Sherman, *Memoirs,* 564–65.

34. OR vol. 44, p. 784.

35. OR vol. 44, pp. 797–98.

36. Sherman, *Memoirs,* 640–44; Marion B. Lucas, *Sherman and the Burning of Columbia* (Columbia: University of South Carolina Press, 2000; originally published by Texas A &M University Press, 1976).

Chapter 10

1. Stanley P. Hurshon, *The White Tecumseh: A Biography of General William T, Sherman* (New York, John Wiley & Sons, 1997), 323. Kennett, *Sherman*, 286–89; Marszalek, *Sherman*, 361–62.

2. Sherman, *Memoirs*, 759–60; Kennett, *Sherman*, 287–92; Marszalek, *Sherman*, 377–78.

3. Kennett, *Sherman*, 298; Marszalek, *Sherman*, 380.

4. Kennett, *Sherman*, 316; Marszalek, *Sherman*, 379.

5. Sherman, *Memoirs*, 760–61; Hirshson, *The White Tecumseh*, 324, 331; Kennett, *Sherman*, 297; Marszalek, *Sherman*, 392; Stephen E. Ambrose, *Nothing Like it in the World* (New York: Simon & Schuster, 2000), 63, 171, 183, 258, 357.

6. Sherman, *Memoirs*, 763; Hirshson, *The White Tecumseh*, 328–29; Kennett, *Sherman*, 283–301; Marszalek, *Sherman*, 364–76.

7. Sherman, *Memoirs*, 787–98; Kennett, *Sherman*, 304; Marszalek, *Sherman*, 384–85.

8. Hirshson, *The White Tecumseh*, 346–47; Marszalek, *Sherman*, 389–99.

9. Kennett, *Sherman*, 309; Kennett, *Sherman*, 308; Marszalek, *Sherman*, 362–63, 386–87.

10. Sherman, *Memoirs*, 799; Marszalek, *Sherman*, 387.

11. Sherman, *Memoirs*, 800–01; Kennett, *Sherman*, 311; Marszalek, *Sherman*, 388–89.

12. Hirshson, *The White Tecumseh*, 343; Kennett, *Sherman*, 316; Marszalek, *Sherman*, 432–44.

13. Sherman, *Memoirs*, 803–10; Hirshson, *The White Tecumseh*, 378–79; Marszalek, *Sherman*, 445–46.

14. "The West Point Holiday," *New York Times*, June 13, 1883.

15. Marszalek, *Sherman*, 446–47.

16. Kennett, *Sherman*, 333; Marszalek, *Sherman*, 447–55.

17. Hirshson, *The White Tecumseh*, 356–57; Kennett, *Sherman*, 319; Marszalek, *Sherman*, 404.

18. Sherman, *Memoirs*, 799; Hirshson, *The White Tecumseh*, 363–68; Kennett, *Sherman*, 326–27; Marszalek, *Sherman*, 401–21.

19. Hirshson, *The White Tecumseh*, 384–85; Kennett, *Sherman*, 334–35; Marszalek, *Sherman*, 479–90.

20. Marszalek, *Sherman*, 490–91.

21. Hirshson, *The White Tecumseh*, 384–85; Kennett, *Sherman*, 336–37; Marszalek, *Sherman*, 491–92.

22. Kennett, *Sherman*, 339–40; Marszalek, *Sherman*, 491–99.

23. B. H. Liddell Hart, *Sherman: Soldier, Realist, American* (New York: Dodd, Mead and Co, 1929; Frederick A. Praeger, New York, 1960).

Index

Fourteenth Corps, 149, 153
Freedman's Bureau, 104
Frémont, John C., 43
Fuller, J.F.C., 178

Garrard, Kenner, 127
Georgia Railroad, 124–5, 127–8
German Americans, 31
Gordon, Ed, 52
Grant, Ulysses S., vii-ix, 3, 4, 10,
    25, 42, 45, 47–50, 54–62,
    64–5, 67–9, 71–9, 82–5, 90,
    92–100, 106–7, 111, 118–19,
    124, 136, 138, 141–3, 146–51,
    153, 160, 162–3, 165–9,
    171–2, 176–7 command of
    Military Division of the
    Mississippi, 93 general-in-chief
    of Union armies, 107 and
    maneuver warfare, 106, 177 as
    president, 168–9, 171–2
    Shiloh, 54–8 and Henry
    Halleck, 58–9 See Vicksburg
    Campaign
Greeley, Horace, 32
Gregg, John, 74
Guderian, Heinz, 178
guerrillas, 60–1, 93, 142

Halleck, Henry W., 10, 17, 43–5,
    47, 49–50, 57–60, 88–9, 92–3,
    123–4, 136–8, 143, 149
Hampton, Wade, 161–2
Hardee, William J., 116, 159
Harrison, William Henry, 8
Hart, Basil H. Liddell, 178
Haynes's Bluff, 73, 76
Hazen, William B., 158–9
Hitchcock, Henry, 152, 154–8
Hood, John Bell, 1–3, 125–8,
    130–1, 133–4, 137–9, 144–50,
    159–60
Hooker, Joseph, 10, 133

Howard, Oliver O., 132–5, 137–8,
    149, 153, 157–8
Hurlbut, Stephen, 49, 100–2

Jackson, Andrew, 82, 167–8
Johnson, Reverdy, 73–4
Johnston, Albert Sidney, 40–1,
    54–5, 59, 116–17
Johnston, Joseph, 2, 74, 83–5,
    108, 110–25, 139, 150, 160,
    162–3

Key, Thomas M., 43
Knoxville Campaign, 99–100

Lancaster, Ohio, 5–8, 12–13, 20–6,
    29–30, 100
land mines, 157–8
Lee, Robert E., x, 107, 119, 142,
    160, 163, 176
Lincoln, Abraham, 27, 29–30, 32,
    39–40, 42, 58, 60–2, 64, 83,
    88–9, 99, 136, 139, 141, 143,
    145, 159, 162
Lincoln, Robert, 173
Logan, John A., 129–32, 172
Longstreet, James, 99
Louisiana Military Seminary, 26–7,
    84
Lucas, James H., 22–5, 29
Lyon, Nathan, 31

Mackenzie, Ranald, S., 170
Mahan, Dennis Hart, 9
maneuver warfare, vii, x, 1–4, 106,
    108, 110, 112–15, 117–23,
    130–2, 139, 150, 177–8
Manifest Destiny, 16
March to the Sea, 4, 152–60, 164,
    177 lead-up to, 146–52
Marcy, Randolph B., 169
Mason, Richard B. 17–19
McClellan, George B., 43, 136

McClernand, John, 49, 54–6, 61, 64–5, 67, 69, 71–2, 74–6, 78–80, 82–3
McDowell, Irvin, 32–7
McPherson, James B., 69, 72, 74–6, 78–9, 81–2, 100–3, 108, 110–12, 119–21, 124–6, 128–33, 138, 152, 172
Meade, George G., 107
Memphis and Charleston Railroad, 48–9, 59, 93
Meridian Campaign, 99–104, 106, 108, 110
Mexican-American War, viii, 15–21
Mexico, 109, 168
military character, viii, 32, 38–45, 50, 53–5, 57, 70–1, 76, 81, 111, 132–3, 137–8, 177–8
Military Division of the Mississippi, 93, 107
military positions adjutant, 17–20 brigadier general, viii, 40, 87 colonel of infantry, viii, 31–2 command of the Army of the Tennessee, 93 command of District of West Tennessee, 60 command of the Military Division of the Mississippi, 107 command of the Military Division of the Missouri, 166 commissary captain, 21–2 first lieutenant, 11 General of the Army, 168–73 lieutenant general, 168 major general of volunteers, 57, 87 quartermaster, 22 second lieutenant, 10 military strategy See maneuver warfare; total warfare
militias, 27–8, 31
Mississippi River, ix, 12, 28, 61, 65, 85
Morgan, George W., 63, 65, 69

Mower, Joseph, 80

Napoleon I of France, 9, 146, 163
Napoleon III of France, 109
Native Americans, 166–7, 169–71
New York City, New York, 24–5, 174–6
New York Tribune, 32, 42–3

Ord, Edward O.C., 10

Panic of 1857, 24–5
Patton, George H., 178
Pemberton, John C., 10, 61–4, 73–6, 106
Pittsburgh Landing, 48–50, 56, 58
Polk, James K., 16
Polk, Leonidas, 101, 110–12, 116–17
Pope, John, 47, 58
Porter, David Dixon, 62, 64–5, 68–70, 72
Prentiss, Benjamin, 49, 52, 54

Rawlins, John A., 71, 80, 168
Reconstruction, 88–9, 166–7
Red River Campaign, 109–10
Red River War, 169–71
Republican party, 26
Richmond, 32–3, 38, 107, 136, 151, 153
Rosecrans, William S., 9, 61, 87, 90, 92–3, 95, 107

St. Louis, Missouri, 21–2, 24–5, 29–31, 44, 47, 165–6, 171, 173–4, 176
San Francisco, California, 18, 22–5, 30
Sanborn, John, 81
Savannah, fall of, 159
Savannah Campaign *See* March to the Sea

Schenck, Robert C., 34
Schofield, John M., 108, 119–21, 125, 128–30, 133, 135, 172
School of Application for Infantry and Cavalry, 172
Scott, Thomas W., 43
Scott, Winfield, 18
secession, viii, 27, 31
Sherman Summit, 167
Siege of Vicksburg, 77–84, 87–8
Seminole Wars, 11–12, 113
Seventeenth Corps, 69, 72, 74, 83, 100–1, 109, 130–1, 134, 149, 153, 157–8
Seward, William H., 39
Sheridan, Philip H., 172, 176
Sherman, Charles Robert (father), 5–6, 8, 24, 176
Sherman, Eleanor ("Ellen") Boyle Ewing (wife), viii, 12–13, 16, 20–6, 30, 42–4, 89–91, 100, 174–6 death of, 175 pregnancies, 21–2, 26, 30 temperament, 22–6, 30, 174–5
Sherman, Eleanor Mary ("Elly") (daughter), 30, 89–91, 176
Sherman, Elizabeth (sister), 6, 25
Sherman, John (brother), 25, 29–30, 43, 176
Sherman, Maria ("Minnie") (daughter), 21, 23, 25–6, 30, 89–91, 175–6
Sherman, Mary Elizabeth ("Lizzie") (daughter), 22–3, 25–6, 30, 89–91, 176
Sherman, Mary Hoyt (mother), 5–6, 8, 10, 12
Sherman, Thomas Ewing ("Tommy") (son), 30, 89–91, 175–6
Sherman, William Ewing ("Willy") (son), 25–6, 30–1, 89–91, 176

Sherman, William Tecumseh ("Cump") and Abraham Lincoln, 29–30, 39–40, 42, 141 banker, viii, 22–5 birth of, 5–6 businessman, 29–30 character, viii, ix, 7–10, 13, 22–4, 26, 44, 104 See also military character childhood, viii, 6–8 correspondence, 3, 42, 50, 71–2, 82, 84, 88–9, 93, 125, 138, 141–5, 147–8, 150–1, 173 criticism of, viii, 137–8, 176 death of, 175–6 death of son, 90–1 and enemy atrocities, 161–2 on enemy populations, 60–2 marriage See Eleanor "Ellen" Boyle Ewing Sherman nervous breakdown, 41–5 nickname "Uncle Billy," 153 and peace agreement, 162–3 on politics, 174 postwar popularity, 163, 165, 171 property manager, 26 on Reconstruction, 88–9 reputation of, vii-ix, 24, 38–44, 53–5, 57, 59, 163, 171 retirement from military, 173–4 school superintendent, 26–8 siblings, 6, 12, 25 trip to Europe, 171 and Ulysses S. Grant, vii-ix, 3, 42, 50, 55, 57–62, 71–9, 82, 85, 90, 93–100, 107, 141–3, 146–51, 162–3, 165–9 wounds, 53, 55 writer, 18–19, 145–6, 174 See maneuver warfare; March to the Sea; military character; military positions; Thirteenth U.S. Infantry; total warfare
Sixteenth Corps, 100–1, 128–30, 134, 166
Sixty-ninth New York brigade, 35–9